COLOUR
YOUR GARDEN

COLOUR YOUR GARDEN

A Portfolio of Inventive Planting Schemes

MARY KEEN

ILLUSTRATIONS BY LIZ PEPPERELL

conran
OCTOPUS

First published in 1991 by
Conran Octopus Limited
2-4 Heron Quays, London E14 4JP

A Part of Octopus Publishing Group

This paperback edition published in 1994
by Conran Octopus Limited

Reprinted in 1997, 1999

British Library Cataloguing in Publication Data
A catalogue record for this
book is available from
the British Library

ISBN 1-85029-586-7

Project Editor	Peggy Vance
Art Editor	Peter Cross
Copy Editor	Barbara Mellor
Editorial Assistant	Helen Ridge
Picture Researcher	Jessica Walton
Illustrators	Liz Pepperell
	David Downton
Production	Jackie Kernaghan

Typeset by Litho Link Ltd, Welshpool, Powys, Wales
Printed in Hong Kong

CONTENTS

INTRODUCTION 6

BLUES 20

REDS 40

GREENS, GREYS *and* WHITES 62

YELLOWS 80

MIXED COLOURS 100

SEASONAL COLOURS 120

PLANT *and* COLOUR DIRECTORIES 136

FURTHER READING *and* ACKNOWLEDGMENTS 144

INTRODUCTION

*C*OLOUR, WHICH IS FLEETING, GIVES A *planting its character, like the expression on a face. Playing with colour in a garden is the nearest most of us will ever come to painting.*

Visions of delphiniums and roses in the rich colours of summer are imprinted on most people's memories. The hazy Salvia sclarea turkestanica, though perhaps less familiar, is no less evocative.

Tulips in the colours of boiled sweets among a mist of blue forget-me-nots are a conventional choice in spring. But in hues of blackcurrant, cherry and lemon, as here, they look both more original and more subtle.

'Colour', said an academic friend, 'is a scientific subject,' implying that this writer would find the technical side of it difficult to master or convey. It is, and I do, but that is beside the point. Just as works of art are the product of more than a knowledge of optical phenomena and music is composed that transcends counterpoint, there is no guarantee that an understanding of how the spectrum works will give you a lovely garden. It would make more sense to say that colour is not so much a scientific subject as a subjective science, and I think this definition is more helpful to the artist gardener than the suggestion that colour is just a set of rules.

Playing with colour and form in the garden is the nearest that most of us will ever get to painting, and the techniques used by

gardeners for combining colours are much simpler than those used by artists. Compared with applying paint to canvas, growing plants is easy. For in a garden the vision of the eye is not limited by the dexterity of the hand in translating it into a solid image. Out of doors, living compositions arrange themselves into perfect pictures, requiring nothing more than inspired censorship on the part of the gardener.

Artists, I suspect, derive more inspiration from looking at paintings or at nature than they do from colour wheels. Similarly, modern gardeners can absorb a sense of what will work from looking at other people's arrangements of plants. The Victorians, who went in for theorizing about colour, produced some associations that would now be considered unsubtle, perhaps

Opium poppies and mallows in all shades of pink, crimson and scarlet make a satisfying summer picture, richer in tone than the clearer, almost transparent colours of spring shown opposite.

A liberal use of white in both the painted trelliswork of the arbour and the flowers chosen allows this gardener to combine magenta, three shades of pink and the odd orange poppy together in a dashing and lavish display.

because of their dependence on science. The research of Dr Brent Elliott, the acknowledged expert on nineteenth-century gardens, has revealed that the theory of complementary colour (developed by Chevreul, the chemist in charge of dyes at the Gobelin tapestry and carpet factory) dominated early Victorian planting. The legacy of complementary colour schemes lingers today. To Chevreul we owe that combination of bright yellow and strong purple that is often found in modern easy-care shrubberies.

Highly charged contrasts like this were however challenged by some Victorians, and most notably by Donald Beaton, the head gardener at Shrubland Park in Suffolk, who turned to horticultural journalism and plant-breeding in later life. Beaton was sympathetic to the ideas of Owen Jones, the architect responsible for the decoration of the Crystal Palace and author of the classic reference work on Victorian ornamental art, *The Grammar of Ornament*. He expressed a preference for designs incorporating all the primary colours in small amounts, balanced and supported by the secondary and tertiary colours in larger masses, which sounds very bright today. Beaton liked to adjust colour schemes in order to take into account any background colour. According to Dr Elliott he praised the yellow calceolarias

Here white is used to different effect. This time it enlivens a picture of greens, greys and receding blues to become the most startling element of the composition. This sort of understated effect belongs to twentieth-century ideas of garden design.

and scarlet geraniums which were used extensively at the Crystal Palace because they compensated for the amount of blue and white already present in the surrounding stonework and the glass of the building. Even allowing for the enormous scale on which Victorian gardeners bedded out, their flat mosaics of colour are less appealing now than the more varied and subtle effects that modern gardeners can create, using flowers of different heights and leaves of varying textures.

Colour harmonies, like musical ones, need careful orchestration, particularly on a small scale – though not perhaps as careful as that practised by the Victorians. We have absorbed their knowledge and progressed beyond it: taste today can allow for what John Sales, Chief Gardens Adviser to the English National Trust, calls 'the Happy Accident'. Like the deliberate mistake said to be sewn into every Persian carpet, our sophisticated colour schemes should not stick too closely to the rules.

Here a blue pavilion in the author's garden, rather than a white one, gives added richness to bright summer colours which are not dissimilar to those opposite. Compare the sparkle of the planting with the white trellis to the moodiness of this one.

Gertrude Jekyll shared an Impressionist, rather than a Victorian, eye for colour in the garden. The Impressionists' vision of softened images which blur into patterns of light and shade is nearer to the way we see things than are the separate and defined blocks of colour so characteristic of both Victorian painting and gardening. Jekyll, like the Victorians, gardened on a scale that is now virtually extinct, but her principles remain useful:

'It is just in the way it is done that lies the whole difference between commonplace gardening and gardening that may rightly claim to rank as a fine art. Given the same space of ground and the same material, they may either be fashioned into a dream of beauty, a place of perfect rest and refreshment of mind and body – a series of soul-satisfying pictures – a treasure of well-set jewels; or they may be so misused that everything is jarring and displeasing. To learn how to perceive the difference and how to do right is to apprehend gardening as a fine art.'

Pictorial gardening is frowned on by those horticulturalists who put plants before colour, and who prefer to grow something rare rather than valuing a flower for its contribution to the picture

A spring composition of clouds of pale pink and white crab apple blossom suspended above white water lilies gives an impression of reflected light.

A different sort of impressionistic effect is produced by harmonizing colours which share the same base, such as these misty lavenders and purple Clematis x jackmanii.

as a whole. At Giverny Monet enjoyed sheets of nasturtiums with plenty of gladioli, as well as sunflowers and lupins side by side. These are not plants about which serious gardeners enthuse. Their search for variety has perhaps been encouraged by the fact that our gardens are nutshell-small. There is no denying that plant collections are fascinating to visit – but to live with? Given the choice between the Royal Horticultural Society's gardens at Wisley and Giverny with attendant gardeners, I would pick Giverny every time. The painterly garden has more to offer the home gardener than a scaled-down museum.

Fitting flowers into a colour composition is no less of a challenge than growing large numbers of rarities. It can even be quite demanding horticulturally: compulsive gardeners can be reassured that colour will keep them fully occupied. Plantsmen put plants where they are most likely to grow; colourists have to bend the rules. No self-respecting horticulturalist would put, say, a phlox and a hebe in the same bed (as in the arrangement on page 57) for the sake of the colour of their flowers, because hebes like it hot and dry while phlox prefer it cool and moist. But

In Monet's own garden at Giverny banked flowers in assorted colours turn into an Impressionist haze only when you stand far away (or look at the picture through squinting eyes).

Opposite left: Startling scarlet lobelias and dahlias in the Red Borders at Hidcote are stimulating in their effect, not restful.

followers of Monet will treat plants as elements in a composition; in a case like this, extra mulching and watering of the phlox would allow them to grow both plants together.

Some might be too squeamish for this sort of manipulation of nature and others will heartily disapprove, but gardens are by definition cultivated and unnatural places where people can play at being God. The Garden of Eden may not have been colour co-ordinated but it was paradise – and one of the quickest routes to paradise in a private garden is to take colour seriously.

Colour, like music, is good at creating moods, and this knowledge of the properties of colour is one of the ways in which we differ from our gardening ancestors. Colour consultants advise hospitals to paint their walls in calming shades such as pale blue, or in cheerful yellows. Why should gardeners not benefit from this sort of trick? If you think this is nonsense think of red flowers, not restful but stimulating, or of blue ones which bring a sense of misty distance into the smallest garden, or of the yellow flowers of jasmine, like sunshine in winter. The challenge out of doors is that colour-induced moods change with the light, even before the flowers fade. You cannot rely on any hue to stay the same throughout the year, or even throughout a day. 'Colour', writes the American painter Robert Dash, who is also a gardener, 'is full of lurking betrayals, so that sky blue becomes sea blue, or slate blue and then not blue at all.'

Painters traditionally choose to work in north-facing studios because they know the effect that light can have on colour. It is a surprising fact that a white handkerchief in the shade may look darker than a lump of coal in sunshine: try it and you will see how deceptive light can be. In shade pale flowers stand out, while in sunlight bright ones fade. Remember too that colours affect one another. At its simplest this can be shown by choosing two shades, bright red and clear blue perhaps. Apart, they keep their separate identities, one cheerful and warm, the other calm and cool. Even if they remain unmixed, when placed next to one another the colours produce not the two original images, but two new ones. They change, becoming heavier and harder. The blue turns slightly mauve and the red becomes a little more crimson as the shades spread towards one another. Add green, as you always

Opposite right: The marginally less strong but still striking reds of bergamot, coleus and Fuchsia 'Thalia' mean that they are not the sort of plants you would choose to include in a calm corner of the garden.

The soothing blues of catmint could not evoke a more different response.

White is used here to 'lift' a deep border, separating the mounds of hot and heavy colours and preventing the planting from looking too leaden.

must in a garden, and they change again. Add masses of white and they separate. If this is beginning to sound complicated then consider too the unreliability of flowers, which come and go as they choose, so that the timing of a set piece can be ruined by the non-appearance of one colour. Arranging colour in the garden is every bit as demanding as growing a few rare plants.

Principles which work for one person will often not be universally applicable, but just as horticulturalists compare the techniques they use to grow difficult plants, so garden colourists should enjoy working out how they can achieve their effects. The point of this book is to provide ideas to analyse, and perhaps some inspiration for those who want to experiment with colour. The plans are designed to be setting-off points, because flower borders are never static, nor can you be sure of being entirely satisfied with what you have set out to do when it is done; adjustments will always need to be made to suit your circumstances or your style.

Like the Victorian head gardener Beaton, you cannot ignore background colour either. Blessed with a brick house in primary red, Beaton might have advocated yellow and blue bedding, however, whereas most of us today would prefer to play down the building with paler shades of secondary colours, like apricot or pink. With Jekyll and Monet's advice on colour similar caution needs to be exercised. For their effects they relied on plenty of temporary colour from hardy and half-hardy annuals and perennials. Such flowers are better at creating colour than almost any others, but they do mean work. At the turn of the century labour was abundant, so they could afford to indulge in masses of these plants. I have included more in the designs than is currently fashionable, but not nearly as many as they would have used. You may prefer to avoid them altogether. I have also suggested plenty of bulbs, the easiest form of temporary colour to manage.

The way to treat the plans is to regard them as a nucleus for your own planting. Some, the ones around which you can walk, might be dropped into a garden setting more easily than others, those which need a wall or a hedge to provide their background.

On the left, Rosa chinensis 'Mutabilis', in shades of coppery pink, is just the rose to put against a wall which combines plum and apricot in its bricks. Colour complements the materials of fixed elements in the garden, providing more fleeting character and atmosphere.

Against the ochre of the walls at Great Dixter (right) Christopher Lloyd plants sulphur-yellow achillea and lacquer-red poppies. Even the darkened timbers of the house are echoed in the poppies' black streaks.

Plenty of good plants have had to be left out, because the range available to modern gardeners is so vast. The plants that I consider most indispensable to any modern scheme are the vertical ones. These are the flowers which will give the illusion of masses of colour crammed into a small space. Climbers will do this too, but the foxgloves, mulleins, delphiniums, aconitums, hollyhocks, salvias and countless others which are repeated throughout the book are not to be lightly discarded. The problem, as always, is not what to put in, but what to leave out. For this reason I find colour easiest to handle in varying harmonies of one primary, with only one very occasional accent of contrast.

As the seasons change so do the appropriate colours, but mixing them in small spaces is harder than in the long borders that Gertrude Jekyll, the arch-colourist, favoured, so I play safe with a restricted palette. Greens in varying shades are as agreeable as any colour in the garden – and because you cannot beat green into submission out of doors you might as well make the most of it occasionally (as on page 74). The only flowers which will subdue green tend to be free-flowering annuals, which is why followers of Monet love them. Some gardeners would recommend coloured foliage rather than annuals as an antidote to green, but for me

Foxgloves and lupins provide vital vertical elements where space is short. They are especially effective against a dark evergreen backdrop, where they seem to stack in towers of creamy yellow.

The deep blue spires of delphiniums and more delicate campanulas are the perfect foil for the flat, pale yellow heads of achillea and yellow wallflowers.

these permanent shades lack the ephemeral delight of flowers.

After a restricted palette, it is a respect for the changing qualities of light throughout the year that helps me to achieve what I want – sometimes. In winter, colours vary between misty and sharp. Then flowers that are yellow or white are valuable because they illuminate dark gardens. The clear light of spring presents colours at their purest, and pale colours come into their own. Rich shades of blues and reds are needed in summer, when the sun bleaches everything but yellows, which it turns brassy. The low light of autumn restores subtlety, encouraging a palette of quite strong colours which in the glare of summer might seem crude. At this late stage of the year, the mellow light also suits tawny browns and oranges.

Colour, which is fleeting, gives a planting its character, like an expression on a face. It is that expression of character and mood in a garden that this book hopes to inspire.

Iris sibirica with sword-like leaves shares the vertical role with foxgloves, alliums and campanulas, while at the same time adding a feeling of depth against a background of varying greens.

BLUES

*B*LUE COOLS ALL COLOURS, ADDING A *sense of space and peace to any composition. But blues come in two moods: the bright ones lift the spirits as a summer sky might do, while the softer, mistier ones spread a wash of gentle melancholy over the garden.*

Airy delphiniums in Cambridge and Oxford blues are ranged behind a free-flowering crane's-bill (Geranium ibericum) which tends towards violet. Blues such as these can be counted on to create an atmosphere of restful, if sometimes melancholy, harmony.

Blue is the colour for distance. Think of mountains far away, or of Claude Lorrain's paintings which have warm brown foregrounds fading to silvery blue, so that you feel you can step into them for miles. A painting is much smaller than a garden: if it is possible to trick people into believing that a canvas six feet by four can lead them into infinite space, then you can use a similar magic to make your garden look as though it goes on for ever. Gertrude Jekyll, who specialized in outsize herbaceous borders, always put blues at the far end. As you walked down their length it must have seemed as though the ribbons of flowers would unroll for ever. A similar illusion is to be found in bluebell woods, where the trees almost seem to be afloat. Could it be this feeling of perpetual motion which lends enchantment to the view?

If it is the property of some blues to lengthen the view and make you stand and dream, others, the clearer hues, have a more immediate effect. Like yellows, the blues come in two cadences, happy and sad: they do not all create the same mood. Positive blue, or blue which is sharpened by white, lifts the spirits as a summer sky or a sight of the azure sea might do. Think of forget-me-nots, or blue-and-white china, or a bright blue dress. The expression 'feeling blue' would probably not call any such

A bluebell wood provides a powerful demonstration of blue's ability to magnify space: as the flowers recede the colours become denser, and the trees seem almost to be afloat on a sea of blue stretching into the distance.

agreeable sights to mind. The melancholy blues are the ones which do not tend to provoke an immediate reaction of pleasure. These are the minor key shades, the twilight lavenders and misty Michaelmas daisies which leave you feeling calm and thoughtful rather than ebullient. While bright blues might be said to induce feelings more appropriate to major key harmonies, the sad blues give to a garden the depth and overall moodiness that you would expect from a minor movement in music.

If I have laboured this point it is to demonstrate that there are as many shades of meaning in a colour as there are tones within its range. And when all that has been said, light, which dissolves and changes everything, will work its magic on blues as it does on all colours, so that in shade even the bright blues will dim and behave as though they are moody ones. Towards the end of the day the blue of forget-me-nots will fade, so that what appeared as a cheerful slice of sky under the midday sun can give an illusion of

Meconopsis, the Himalayan blue poppy, makes a dramatic blue pool. It is difficult to combine with calmer blues because it has a tendency towards turquoise, which brings an electric charge to its setting.

By covering sections of this picture you can see the effect that bright yellow and grey have on the blue of the catmint at the centre. Cut out the yellow and it is dimmed; cut out the grey and it instantly becomes more stimulating.

depth and distance late in the afternoon. And if you stick to a hazy palette, that too will change with the light, for in the sun the colour will be richer and will echo the languorous pace of a hot day, while in shade it will be greyer and cooler. Think of cornflowers in bright sunshine and then think of lavender. The first image produces a sharper effect, like the colours which people wear by the sea. The second is heavier, almost like a violet sky before a thunderstorm. Then think of both plants in shade, where the lavender becomes greyer and less sensual and the cornflowers, so unaffected and cheerful in the sunshine, are transformed into something mysterious and cool.

In order to stage a mirage effect you might, then, choose to use clear blues in shade, or the soft grey and hazy purple ones to lead the eye on in sun – remembering perhaps that while clear blues remain stimulating in shade, on grey days the lavender-blues can look very doleful indeed. To intensify any blue, avoid too many dark green leaves and choose glaucous or silver ones instead. With misty shades this might tend to give you a fit of the blues under sullen skies, so you might like to lean more heavily on silver than on blue-green leaves, or even add a dash of white to lighten it all. But then you would be sacrificing your illusion of distance.

Van Gogh said, 'There is no blue without yellow and orange, and when you paint blue, paint yellow and orange as well.' It is true that if not placed near a contrasting colour blue seems almost negative, like the absence of colour, which is perhaps why it is so good at creating a mirage effect. But if, like van Gogh, you want to appreciate the blueness of blue then you need to follow his advice and use yellow or orange to define the colour. One of the best illustrations of this can be seen in the painter John Hubbard's garden, where orange marigolds and blue felicia edge a narrow path. Non-colourists might not, however, want to take their experiment that far, for flowers somehow cease to be flowers when they are used in such broad brush strokes. Gertrude Jekyll, whose early training as an artist encouraged her to explore the use of colour in the garden, wrote that 'any experienced colourist knows that blues will be more telling – more purely blue – by the juxtaposition of rightly placed complementary colour'. In a

Compare the soothing range of blue and white delphiniums with its edging of catmint, on the left, with the brighter effect of the Barnsley House tulips on the right. Just as painters and interior designers often use a touch of red to bring a design to life, so a splash of scarlet in the garden gives a refreshing jolt to the senses.

'Forget-me-nots with red tulips provide another exercise in the way colours affect each other: cover the white, then block the red, and finally look at the whole picture to see how the forget-me-nots change their blue with each different combination.

scheme for a blue garden she used citron and canary yellow lupins with snapdragons, as well as white lilies and tree lupins, to set off what she called 'pure blues'. No purple blues, like the bluest of the campanulas and the perennial lupins, were to be included, for 'they would not be admissible', she ruled. It may be that an exception to Monet and Jekyll's rule should be made for meconopsis, the Himalayan blue poppy. In some forms, such as *Meconopsis × sheldonii*, the blue is so intense and luminous that it can stand alone. Indeed it is a difficult colour to combine with others in the same range, and there is something to be said for enjoying this meconopsis in a woodland setting unaccompanied by other flowers, which only dilute or vulgarize its impact. Hydrangeas grown on acid soil present similar problems, for their piercing blue tends to look synthetic against plants which flower in quieter tones.

Opposite: Van Gogh said, 'When you paint blue, paint yellow as well.' Here yellow achillea intensifies the blue of the delphiniums, just as he recommended.

28 BLUES

Innocent blues belong most of all to spring, when the limpid light suits their clarity and the pallor of fresh leaves provides enough yellow to balance the blue. 'Blue and green should ne'er be seen' goes the old saying, but provided the green veers towards yellow rather than blue, it is easy to dispel this prejudice. The pale green bottlebrushes of *Euphorbia characias* work better with the bright blue of scillas, for example, than would the dark leaves of evergreens like yew or box.

In any composition of green and blue the balance is a difficult one. The two colours share the same primary base, which tends to deaden the blue when they are used together. Lightening the green until it becomes almost yellow will bring the blue back to life again. Putting a pale blue flower against a dark green hedge would produce a different effect. Here the balance is more a question of value than of hue, as the colours of the plants do not compete with one another at all. Pale blue against dark green produces what appears to be no more than a contrast of light and dark, whereas with the euphorbia and the scillas what you notice first is not the definition of light and shade but the different colours of the plants.

In high summer, when leaves are darker, blue and green are hard to manage in the same bed. They look dull together because their range of tones is too similar. Introducing white or pale yellow flowers can help, or where you want more permanent light relief, silver or variegated leaves may be the answer. In summer, without the addition of some yellow or orange, a predominantly blue border will have a deadening effect unless green leaves are sharpened to lime, white or silver. The negative properties of blue can work in the gardener's favour, on the other hand, when used to temper hot colour schemes. For blue is the most cool and restful of all the colours, adding a sense of space and calm to any composition.

Blues and Purples

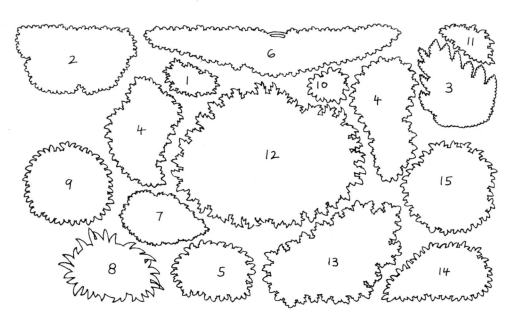

Suggested underplanting throughout: *Narcissus* 'Thalia', *Tulipa* 'Queen of Night', *Aquilegia vulgaris* or *A. alpina* (columbine) and *Verbena bonariensis*

Intense blues and black-purples make an unusual spring colour scheme without any yellow from the daffodil tribe. (Early-mid)

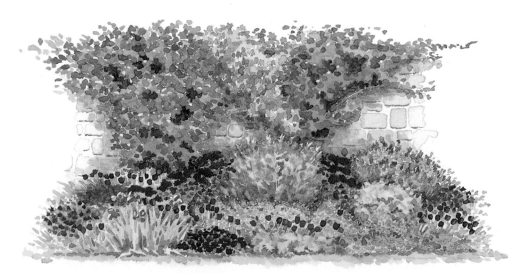

Early

1   *Clematis alpina* 'Frances Rivis'

Early-mid

2   *Ceanothus impressus*
3   *Rosmarinus officinalis* 'Severn Sea'
4   *Lunaria annua* (honesty) underplanted with *Anemone* x *hybrida* 'Honorine Jobert' (mid-late)
5   *Viola* 'Huntercombe Purple'

Mid

6   *Rosa* 'Albéric Barbier'
7   *Linum perenne* (flax)
8   *Iris pallida pallida*, syn. *I. p. dalmatica*
9   *Erysimum* 'Bowles' Mauve'

Mid-late

10   *Clematis* 'Perle d'Azur'
11   *Clematis* x *jackmanii*
12   *Romneya coulteri* (California tree poppy) underplanted with myosotis (forget-me-not) and *Scilla siberica* (both early)
13   *Geranium* 'Johnson's Blue' (crane's-bill)

Late

14   *Aster* x *thompsonii* 'Nanus' underplanted with *Anemone blanda* (early)
15   *Ceratostigma willmottianum*

It is received wisdom that you should not combine colours which share the same primary, as for instance pink and purple or pink and orange do. But sticking to the rules can mean you miss a lot of thrills. Zinnias do not represent everyone's idea of an attractive range of colours because they run through all the half shades from orange to purple. I love them. But while I admit that some might baulk at the zinnia spectrum, which embraces shocking pink, dusty rose, burnt orange and lacquer red, I cannot understand why the combination of purple and blue is another official no-no. If the purple is rich, the blue can vary from clear to misty, which will surely offend no one.

In spring, when other gardens are full of egg-yolk yellow, this border looks unusual. During the summer the creamy 'Albéric Barbier' rose and the blue clematis act as caretakers while nothing much else is out, but the bed comes into its own again at the end of the year, with patches of blue and white flowers until the frosts fall. This means there should be a good spread of colour for five months of the year, split into two periods in spring and late summer, as well as a little interest in high summer from the rose and the

indefatigable 'Perle d'Azur', a clematis which appears in other places in this book because it has such an exceptionally long flowering season.

Bulbs are an important ingredient because they bring early colour to the bed, but the scillas will need renewing or lifting every year because they will not enjoy being under the heavy skirts of the romneya. The anemones should survive if you can make them comfortable in rich but well-drained soil, which will also suit the black-purple tulips. If these are planted deeply you can usually bank on keeping them from year to year. Against a backdrop of rich blue

Erysimum

'Bowles' Mauve'

The bed has a second season with plenty of white flowers from the tree poppy and anemones to add to the blues and purples of clematis and verbena. (Mid-late)

Geranium

'Johnson's Blue'

ceanothus and the pale blue early clematis 'Frances Rivis' they look stunning. At the same time as all these, there should be more blue from the brightest of the rosemaries. This is doubtfully hardy, but is worth a warm corner for the sake of its Aegean-blue flowers which often appear both at the beginning and the end of the year. For the purple team, the perennial wallflower 'Bowles' Mauve' flowers for weeks on end as soon as the weather starts to warm up. It makes a handsome grey bush but can fall apart with the weight of age, so it is best renewed every year from spring cuttings which can replace the parent in the autumn.

If there were room to add *Abutilon* × *suntense* I would, for the sake of its purple flowers, but space is too tight. Honesty produces a dilemma. A very dark purple form enters into the spirit of the planting, but if it all seems too funereal then the variegated white form is the one to choose. Honesty and late summer white anemones must share the same quarters: when the honesty is over uproot the plants because they

Viola

'Blue Gem'

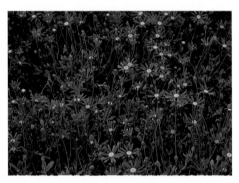

Felicia amelloides

■

tend to get mildew, but remember to save and sow some seed for the following year.

In every available pool of earth forget-me-nots can grow, and between these and throughout the borders unimproved aquilegias in navy-purple should be allowed to appear. Brilliant plantspersons will manage to keep and increase the pure blue *Aquilegia alpina*, which is not nearly so sinister but requires dedication.

The blue and purple theme can be kept going beyond the spring with 'Johnson's Blue' geranium and 'Huntercombe Purple' violas. The airy blue perennial flax is short-lived but worth encouraging. In late summer the thugs move forward. But the Californian tree poppy is so breathtaking that it can be forgiven its oppressive tendencies, and Japanese anemones – which are similarly pushy once they become established – will also see the summer out with plenty of white flowers. Which may be a relief for some who do not share my taste for the deep purple blues.

Scilla siberica

'Atrocaerulea'

Iris pallida pallida

(syn. *I. p. dalmatica*)

Viola

'Huntercombe Purple'

Blue with Silver and Apricot

Early-mid

1 *Eremurus spectabilis* (foxtail lily) or
   Onopordum acanthium (Scotch thistle)
2 *Nectaroscordum siculum*, syn. *Allium
   siculum* (onion)

Mid

3 *Rosa* 'Alchymist'
4 *Artemisia arborescens* or *Teucrium
   fruticans* (tree germander)
5 *Eryngium* x *oliverianum* (sea holly)
6 *Digitalis purpurea* 'Sutton's Apricot'
7 *Nepeta* 'Six Hills Giant' (catmint)
8 *Stachys byzantina* 'Silver Carpet'
9 *Limnanthes douglasii*
10 *Iris pallida pallida*, syn. *I. p. dalmatica*
11 *Hosta plantaginea* (August lily)

Mid-late

12 *Acanthus balcanicus*, syn. *A. longifolius*
13 *Buddleja* 'Lochinch'
14 *Rosa* 'Gloire de Dijon'
15 *Hibiscus syriacus* 'Blue Bird'
   underplanted with *Chionodoxa luciliae*
   (glory of the snow/early)
16 *Crocosmia* 'Citronella' (montbretia)
17 *Geranium wallichianum* 'Buxton's
   Variety'
18 *Rosa* 'Pearl Drift'
19 *Convolvulus sabatius*, syn.
   C. mauritanicus
20 *Mimulus aurantiacus* (monkey flower)

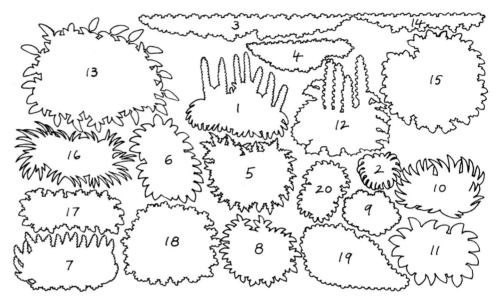

Suggested underplanting throughout: *Narcissus* 'W. P. Milner' and *Tulipa* 'Purissima'

Blue with silver leaves and touches of apricot or warm yellow makes a very different picture from the superficially similar pale blue and yellow angle border shown on pages 94-5. The impression here is one of richness rather than clarity, and this is one of the few colour schemes which bright modern bricks will not harm. There may be little to see in the cold months, but throughout the summer the chosen colours will dominate.

Several plants have been selected for their long flowering season. From late summer through to autumn the hibiscus and the buddleia will be charged with blue blossom; the low-growing *Convolvulus sabatius* is seldom without a blue flower in summer and the nepeta is similarly obliging. With the exception of the catmint, these mainstays demand warmth and shelter to perform well. They are not plants for cold places, but good drainage will improve their chances of survival.

Roses are reliable performers, too, particularly the low-growing 'Pearl Drift', which has glossy leaves and flat pinky-white flowers. This and *R.* 'Alchymist' have the look of old-fashioned roses combined with the modern ability to flower for long periods. 'Alister Stella Gray', or the 'Golden Rambler', is one of the few old roses (it dates from 1894) which is repeat-flowering, and 'Gloire de Dijon' is equally prolific. Mixed summer borders are incomplete without roses, whose silky petals add a gentle texture to any planting.

A constant silver theme keeps the blues charged with life. The buddleia has whitened undersides to its leaves and the stachys makes a woolly grey mat at the front of the border. This form has large leaves and never flowers, which is an improvement on the basic version. At the back, *Artemisia arborescens* will climb through the stems of the rose on warmest walls only. A safer alternative, if slightly less silver, is the tree germander, *Teucrium fruticans*. Left to its own devices this is an untidy bush, but it can be trained on a wall where its small blue flowers will appear among grey leaves all summer. Late in the year, metallic blue thistle flowers appear on the eryngium, adding a spiky note to the picture.

Vertical accents are provided by the curious greenish *Nectaroscordum siculum*, apricot foxgloves and the lilac flower spikes of the noble acanthus. Nearer the front of the bed the glaucous fans of *Iris pallida* make a useful break in shape, echoed by the green spears of the yellow-orange crocosmia. The foxtail lily, which is not the easiest of plants to please, also has strap-shaped leaves, but the point of the struggle to grow it is the great

Nepeta

'Six Hills Giant' (catmint)

Convolvulus sabatius

(syn. *C. mauritanicus*)

spikes of amber-coloured flowers which appear in early summer. Just as spectacular in this position, but not as tricky, would be a plant of the giant Scotch thistle. This dramatic silver biennial begins to look seedy as it flowers, and would be best removed to make way for the eryngium before it loses its sheen and collapses. It is not difficult to grow from seed and, like a giant exclamation mark, always attracts attention.

The pale green leaves of *Hosta plantaginea* provide a different but no less important foil to the other colours. Hostas are good at bringing the eye to rest in a border but are not generally candidates for hot places, except for H. *plantaginea*, the August lily, which has the bonus of scented white flowers in late summer.

Rosa

'Alchymist'

Clematis

'Jackmanii Superba'

Stachys byzantina

(syn. *S. olympica*)

Nectaroscordum siculum

■

Early in the year the yellowed pinks of roses and apricot foxgloves stand out above the rounded mounds of leaves. On the wall, behind the spires of eremurus, appear the buff-apricot petals of Rosa 'Gloire de Dijon'. This rose was a favourite with the Victorians, who loved it for its scent and flopping habit. It is not as vigorous as the later-flowering and yellower variety 'Alister Stella Gray'. (Mid)

In late summer, when cool colours are most welcome, this border of blues and pale apricots comes into its own. Hibiscus and buddleia dominate the planting, but silvery leaves and creamy roses also make an important contribution, while the architectural columns of acanthus add grandeur to the scheme. This is a group for a sunny corner, but one which is not much seen in winter. (Mid-late)

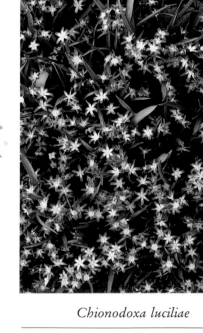

Chionodoxa luciliae

(glory of the snow)

Blue Annuals

Early

1 *Iris pallida pallida*, syn. *I. p. dalmatica*

Mid

2 *Anchusa capensis* 'Blue Angel'
3 *Nemophila menziesii*, syn. *N. insignis* (baby blue-eyes) or *Nigella damascena* 'Miss Jekyll' (love-in-a-mist)
4 *Viola* 'Boughton Blue'
5 *Veronica* 'Blue Fountain'
6 *Dianthus* 'Musgrave's Pink' (old-fashioned pink) or *Dianthus* 'Haytor White' (modern pink)

Mid-late

7 *Felicia amelloides* or *Aster* x *thompsonii* 'Nanus' (late)
8 *Phacelia campanularia* (California bluebell)
9 *Echium lycopsis* 'Blue Bedder', syn. *E. plantagineum* (viper's bugloss)

Late

10 *Ceratostigma plumbaginoides*

Permanent feature

11 *Rosmarinus officinalis* 'Miss Jessopp's Upright' (rosemary)

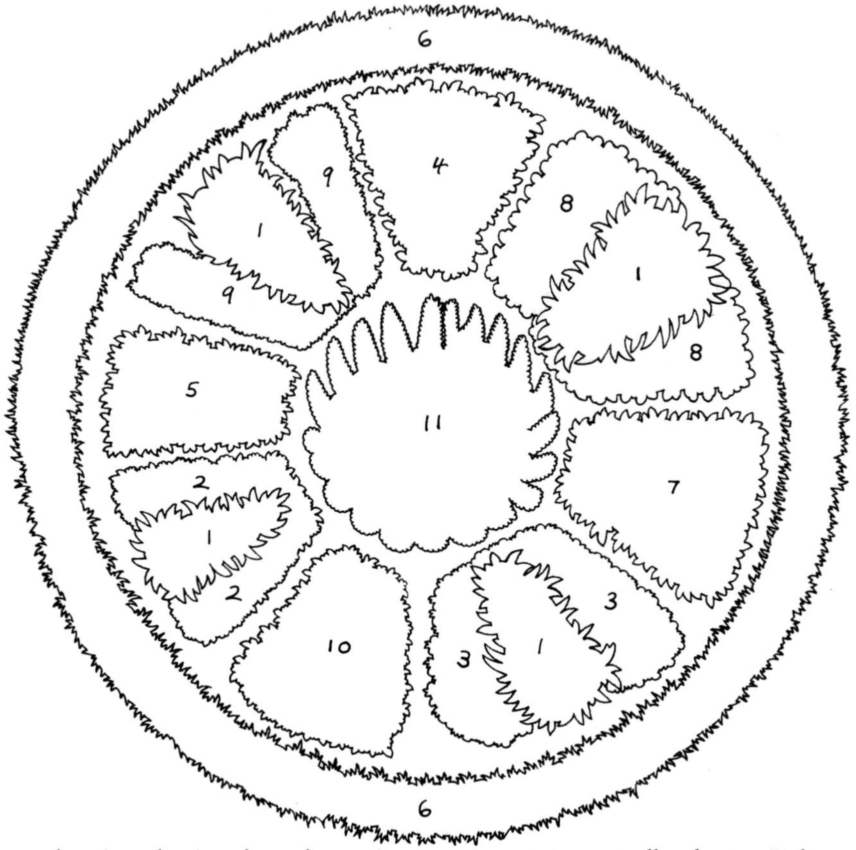

Suggested spring planting throughout: *Crocus tommasinianus*, *Scilla siberica*, *Tulipa* 'Schoonoord' and *Myosotis* 'Blue Ball' (forget-me-not)

*B*edding plants are so expensive that I always wonder why people who like plenty of colour in the summer garden do not try growing annuals in patches among long-flowering perennials. This round flowerbed was inspired by a similar planting at Crathes Castle in Scotland where there is a tradition of annual borders. Inverewe on the west coast of Scotland is famous for another good annual border, which has occasionally used the blue echium, nemophila and nigella seen here, as well as other long-flowering blue summer favourites such as cornflowers, among golden nasturtiums. If you wanted to intensify the blue along colourist lines, a mixture of creamy yellow and blue might form the basis for a variation on the plan shown here, which is a simple colour wheel of blues and greys.

At the hub of the circle is the 'Miss Jessopp's Upright' rosemary, which makes a neat cylindrical evergreen bush with washy-blue flowers in spring and sometimes again in autumn. Like all rosemaries it needs an annual clip to keep it from becoming too woody at the base, best done as the flowers fade.

Annuals are plants of little structure, but this is remedied by the shape of the bed, which gives them a strong framework. The height of the rosemary and the edging of long-flowering *Dianthus* 'Haytor White' also help to give structure. If the circle were bigger it might be possible to run spokes of the dianthus back to the centre, to give each plant its own compartment. As it is the patches of *Iris pallida* make a good substitute for little hedges; they act as breaks between the masses of blue and their lilac flowers help to cover the transition between tulips and annuals. But it is for their greyish leaves that they are most valuable: this is the only iris which can be relied on to stay tidy throughout the summer.

The permanent clumps of low-growing blue plants are almost all reliable and long-flowering. The felicia is not strictly hardy, except in well-drained and very sunny places, but it is no trouble to take one or two cuttings late in the season. They strike easily and can live on the kitchen windowsill. If this sounds daunting the veronica might be repeated, or the little late-flowering *Aster × thompsonii* 'Nanus',

though this is a shade too mauve to keep company with the pure blues of the other plants.

The viola would prefer a place out of the sun and should be positioned in the shadow of the rosemary. This paragon among plants flowers for three months, after which it needs an enforced rest: you can ensure this by shearing the plant to the ground. If this is followed by several buckets of water in a dry season, as well as a course of liquid feed, the viola will be up and flowering again before the month is out.

All the annuals here are easy, and in temperate climates could be sown before the winter so that they get away to an early start; but autumn-sowing would rule out forget-me-nots and tulips because there is not room for them all together. It should be possible to enjoy early crocus, followed by scillas among a few forget-me-nots and

the double white 'Schoonoord' tulip. Three weeks after these have flowered the annuals should be sown directly into the ground. This upheaval would need to be timed to coincide with the flowering of the irises and the rosemary. The viola will also help to provide interest while the annuals are growing. The fastest of the annuals is phacelia, which can be relied on to flower within six weeks of sowing; the rest take a little longer, but once ready they and the felicia should perform until the end of the summer.

Dead-heading is essential, because if they are allowed to set seed their rate of flowering will slow down and then stop. This is a chore, but worth it for the sake of a flowerbed that is much more original than the usual geraniums and lobelias. And if that alone is not enough of a temptation, think of the money that will be saved.

Veronica

'Blue Fountain'

The round bed at Crathes Castle provides the inspiration for the blue and grey colour wheel opposite.

REDS

*A*LL REDS ADD DRAMA TO A BORDER.
*Scarlet, crimson, magenta, cerise and orange
bring life to any planting, for flowers in these
colours are exciting. Their vivid hues clamour for
attention: reds are not for peaceful settings.*

*Jazzy reds and pinks have the opposite
effect to blues in the garden: use their
colours to enliven a planting, but not to
calm or soothe.*

The famous Red Borders at Hidcote, above, are based on an uncompromisingly hot palette. They make an original and startling composition, but might not be everyone's first choice of colour scheme where the available space is more limited.

*I*t is easy to dispute the emotional values of colour, and many people would deny that a particular shade might be expected to evoke a specific mood: to them it would sound silly to say that yellow flowers tend to make people cheerful, or that blue ones seem mysterious. In their view the study of colour is about the relationships of one hue to another and nothing more. It might interest them to think about, say, combining pink and blue for the sake of an attractive border, but claims that colour can reach the psyche leave them cold. Advertising agents know better: they rely on colour to make subliminal suggestions all the time. Green is used to convince people of a product's freshness, while orange or red are meant to stimulate or excite them. On another level western painters have traditionally used blue to suggest spirituality, while red is the colour of temporal power. If this sounds less than convincing when applied to flowers, think of red. Few people can claim to feel relaxed within sight of a red border. Red flowers may startle, excite or impress, but they rarely soothe.

Opposite: This brilliant combination of primary colours — 'Avebury Crimson' oriental poppies and blue anchusa — would have gladdened a Victorian colourist's heart. It may, however, be too strong a combination for some modern tastes.

Where there is no shortage of quieter, cooler or prettier plantings, red borders can form a striking feature, as they do at Hidcote. But this sort of dramatic effect is not easy to live with day in day out. A pure red border is fun if you have the room and can find peace in another part of the garden, but could be overpowering in a small setting. A mixture of red hues clamours for attention, and is not easily ignored.

One of the problems with red is that it looks particularly harsh against the average green of summer leaves. Compare a holly tree, where the berries appear against a blackish-green background, with a bed of scarlet geraniums and you will find that the red of the geraniums is much less restful to the eye than the scarlet of the berries. This is because the geranium leaf has too much yellow in it to quieten the red. Blues soothe and cool reds, while yellows make them more exciting, so choosing varieties with bluish leaves can help if you want to enjoy scarlet without bruising the retina.

The nasturtium *Tropaeolum majus* 'Empress of India' is a good example of this subduing effect: if you put it next to a variety with flowers of the same colour but with light green leaves, you can see what a difference the slightly glaucous background makes to the impact of the lacquer-red nasturtiums.

Red is a quarrelsome colour, and if it is tinted with the other primaries the results are better kept apart. This is less true of blue. When blue is mixed with yellow to produce a greenish blue, and with red to create a dim violet, the two resulting blues are not offensive together, especially when they are seen against a background of green. But a similar process involving mixtures of yellow-red and blue-red would be much more hazardous. These colours, even at their darkest, can make awkward or surprising neighbours. A rich pink rose like 'Constance Spry', for instance, would not be improved by an underplanting of marigolds. But if the rose were 'Albertine', which has a coppery tendency, the combination would be less upsetting. It is sometimes possible to mix yellow-reds with very dark, almost black, blue-reds, like the climbing rose 'Guinée', or the chocolate-scented *Cosmos atrosanguineus*, because of the difference in the relative strengths of the colours. But on the whole pale pink will enhance these

velvety maroons better than salmon-pink can ever do. The pale salmon-pink dianthus 'Doris' is popular, but less flattering to old roses which lack yellow in their make-up than to those which have a few salmon streaks in their petals.

Gardens are more often designed for rest than for excitement, but there are times when a clash of bright colours can be a tonic. Shocking pink and orange flowers in the same bed would not please all tastes, and such bright hues rarely suit temperate zones where the prevailing light is soft. But in the glare of the Mediterranean sun clashes and contrasts often work well. Just as people tend to wear brighter clothes in tropical places, so gardens can afford to take risks under hot suns. Gauguin colours may not suit English gardens, where pastel colours seem to look best, but they can look wonderful in an exotic setting.

The Gauguin colours of azaleas in full flower and a mass of candelabra primulas bring an exotic touch to an English woodland garden.

Scarlet Lychnis chalcedonica *combines an exciting flash of red with the magenta of its cousin* L. coronaria, *whose own colour is toned down by its silvery leaves. The mauve of the linaria adds a cooling touch of blue.*

In traditional gardens, where jazzy clashes seem out of place, deepening the colours can provide a more dignified sort of stimulus. Think of the rich tones of cardinals' robes, or of scarlet and black uniforms: these produce quite a different response from the circus associations of bright pinks and oranges. Scarlet and purple flowers can make a grand statement in a large garden, but may be overpowering in small spaces. Much cosier in a confined area are the cottage colours of crimson and pink, and it is interesting to compare the effects of these different combinations in the same tonal range.

Bland and undemanding, pink is traditionally a colour for baby girls and angels. Pink is too good to be true. In excess even the

inoffensive can be cloying, and pastel shades unsupported by a bolder colour can look weak in the garden. At that moment in early summer when pink often prevails you need to be careful. But pastel shades can be spiked with bright ones and brought to life by the addition of darker colours in the same range. This is a more original way to treat them than the familiar technique of using pale colours to tone down bright ones. Sweet williams are a good illustration of this way of combining colours in one range. Pink, white and crimson are intermingled, producing a much more vibrant mixture than the same colours would make if used more conventionally in larger patches. An illustration of this second method could be drawn from a group including a rich

The purpled reds of old-fashioned roses and pinks are less sombre with the addition of white foxgloves, here demonstrating their uncanny ability to float as if weightless against a dark background.

crimson rose like 'Mme Isaac Pereire', with two sorts of violas in lavender-pink and white growing at its feet. Here the colours flow along separately and appear much quieter. In a mixed composition like the sweet williams they appear brighter and fresher, rather like a piece of spotted material. If you imagine the difference between broad splashes of pinks, reds and whites printed on a piece of cotton and the same colours laid on in spots, you have an idea of how grouping colours can affect the picture in a flowerbed.

An even more restricted way of using red is to treat it as an isolated accent. Just as white or yellow can be relied on to lighten a border, so red can be summoned to inject some life into a planting. Like the *coup de rouge* in a painting, a touch of red can warm up a dull border. Interior decorators often introduce a little red into a room to bring it alive, and the same principle can be followed in the garden. Red is the stimulant which startles and wakes the eye, but like all stimulants it needs to be handled carefully and treated with respect.

Strong Reds

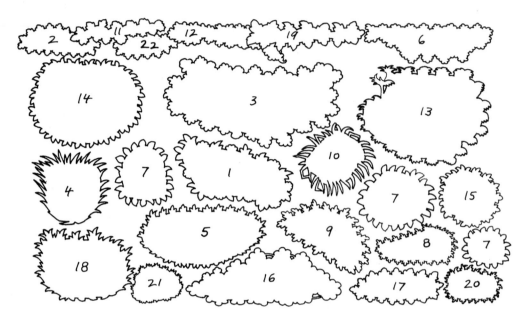

Suggested underplanting throughout: *Tulipa* 'Generaal de Wet' and *T. praestans*

Early

1 *Cheiranthus cheiri* 'Vulcan' (wallflower) followed by *Dahlia* 'Bishop of Llandaff' (mid-late)
2 *Ribes speciosum*

Mid

3 *Rosa moyesii*
4 *Crocosmia* 'Lucifer' (montbretia)
5 *Salvia officinalis* 'Purpurascens' (purple sage)
6 *Geum* 'Mrs Bradshaw'
7 *Rosa chinensis* 'Mutabilis'
8 *Centranthus ruber* (valerian)
9 *Helianthemum* 'Ben Hope' (rock rose)
10 *Knautia macedonica*
11 *Kniphofia caulescens* (red-hot poker) or *Hemerocallis* 'Stafford' (day lily)

Mid-late

12 *Rhodochiton atrosanguineum*
13 *Lonicera* x *brownii* 'Dropmore Scarlet' (honeysuckle)
14 *Foeniculum vulgare* 'Purpureum' (bronze fennel)
15 *Phygelius aequalis* 'Indian Chief' or *Polygonum amplexicaule*
16 *Fuchsia* 'Riccartonii'
17 *Tropaeolum majus* 'Empress of India'
18 *Heuchera micrantha* 'Palace Purple'

Late

19 *Aster lateriflorus* 'Horizontalis'
20 *Vitis vinifera* 'Purpurea' (grapevine)
21 *Cosmos atrosanguineus*
22 *Potentilla atrosanguinea*

The rich reds and purples of cardinals' robes are the inspiration for this group of flowers. A brick wall or a copper beech hedge might make a good backing for this choice of plants, which will need shelter and warmth to keep them at their best – otherwise there is a risk of losing the phygelius and the kniphofia. Alternatives for cooler places might be *Polygonum amplexicaule* and *Hemerocallis* 'Stafford' which, though they might lack the drama of the other two, could be relied on to produce flowers in the right colour over a long period. It would definitely be a pity not to be able to include the kniphofia, because its narrow bluish leaves are handsome in winter. With the coloured stems and hips of *Rosa moyesii* and the purple leaves of the sage, it makes a respectable grouping.

Purple leaves feature throughout this planting, but unless they are kept in check they may ultimately outweigh the clear reds. The fennel, sage, vine and heuchera are also all rampant spreaders, so constant vigilance is needed to keep the balance of the mixture right. The purple sage should be cut back hard when the frosts are over and will probably need renewing every third year. Fennel can spread itself widely, and this middle-aged tendency needs to be dealt with by vicious chopping of extra roots. The single scarlet dahlia 'Bishop of Llandaff' also has purple leaves, adding another dark accent to the arrangement. This dahlia does survive moderate winters in the ground, but it is better lifted and stored for the winter. It likes a rich diet and needs

Crocosmia

'Lucifer'

The scarlets and purples of kniphofia, Lobelia cardinalis, *berberis and* Heuchera *'Palace Purple' make a rich and well-balanced composition. The addition of any more purple to this group might result in crowding out the reds.*

plenty of water in dry summers in order to flower well. The centres of the flower turn yellow with age, and some might prefer to dead-head them early in order to avoid this dilution of pure red. Others may be less fussy, but it is worth remembering that attention to details like this is important if concentrated effects are required.

Another detail worth insisting on for carefully stage-managed colour borders is the pursuit of the right variety to give the desired effect. Here the only valerian to tolerate is the red one. There are dark and pale pink forms as well as white ones, but the only variety that will look right in this instance has a flower which inclines not to purple, but to coral. This is essential, because some of the other reds in the border have a tendency to yellow rather than to blue. The *Rosa chinensis* for example would be particularly off key with anything but pure or orange-reds. It is a curious shot-silk affair of copper and flame, which looks dreadful with mauvish pinks. When deep purple appears later in the year in the fuchsia flowers it is acceptable because, like the purple leaves, the dark colour enriches and brightens the neighbouring reds. Pale mauve, however, would tend to muddy rather than clarify the colours.

Red stops the eye and foreshortens the view, so a planting like this should not be allowed to dominate any outlook from the house. It would be better reserved for a part of the garden that is off the main axis, where it would provide a burst of vibrant colour for occasional visits rather than a confrontation every day. Giving red flowers pride of place in a small garden is a little like painting the front door red. It could be a mistake.

Clear Pinks and Crimsons

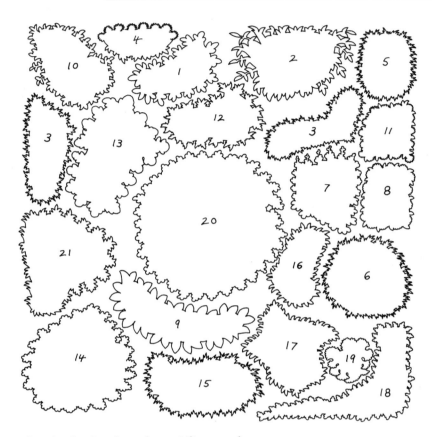

Suggested underplanting throughout: *Lilium regale*

Early-mid

1 *Paeonia officinalis* 'Rubra Plena' (peony)

2 *Prunus tenella* 'Fire Hill' underplanted with *Viola cornuta alba*

3 *Dianthus barbatus* auricula-eyed (sweet william)

Mid

4 *Crepis incana* (pink dandelion)

5 *Dianthus* 'Brympton Red'

6 *Dianthus* 'Dad's Favourite'

7 *Sidalcea* 'Loveliness'

8 *Saponaria officinalis* 'Rosea Plena' (soapwort)

9 *Digitalis purpurea alba* (white foxglove)

Mid-late

10 *Fuchsia* 'Mme Cornelissen'

11 *Osteospermum ecklonis*, syn. *Dimorphotheca ecklonis* (cape marigold)

12 *Geranium endressii* 'Wargrave Pink'

13 *Alcea rosea* 'Nigra', syn. *Althaea rosea* 'Nigra' (hollyhock)

14 *Rosa* 'The Fairy'

15 *Dianthus* 'Haytor White' (modern pink)

16 *Penstemon* 'Garnet'

17 *Antirrhinum* 'Crimson Monarch'

18 *Verbena* 'Silver Anne'

19 *Petroselinum crispum* (parsley)

20 *Rosa* 'Ferdinand Pichard'

21 *Salvia microphylla neurepia*

*T*his square patch of cottage garden flowers illustrates the way in which spiking pink and white with red can make a lively but friendly colour scheme. The broken colours of the striped 'Ferdinand Pichard' rose, the sweet williams and the old-fashioned dianthus all provide the inspiration for a cheerful mixture. There are some dark crimsons from the cottage peony early in the year, and late in the season the same dark note is struck by the maroon hollyhock. These save the planting from being too predictable.

Winter interest has been sacrificed to abundance in summer. Flowers need to be packed to create a cottage look, and the number of plants may be increased by adding more white violas in every space, especially in places where they can take over from early-flowering groups. The sweet williams could either be left to be smothered by violas or removed to make way for more penstemons, which might be white to add to the deep-red 'Garnet'.

Peony leaves are handsome in themselves, but if more flowers were wanted they might be used to provide support for the perennial white lathyrus. This is an effective trick, but the pea does need some management to keep it from smothering its neighbours. It makes a surprisingly late appearance, remaining out of sight until the peony

Cherry red and clear pink spiked with plenty of white form the basis of this cottage garden patch, inspired by the colours of auricula-eyed sweet williams. (Mid)

Later in the summer, reds darken and dominate the centre of the bed. Wine-red penstemons and maroon-black hollyhocks are toned down by the grey domes of dianthus. (Mid-late)

is well past flowering, but then seems to gather strength, and if prevented from setting seed will flower until the end of summer.

For such a small area the flowering season is long, starting with the prunus which bears wands of pink blossom in early spring. This is a shrub which can become ungainly if left unpruned; the roses too will need clever pruning and a rich diet to encourage maximum flowering. Cottage gardens, which may appear to have been artlessly thrown together, are demanding to maintain: where so many plants are expected to give of their best, conditions must be lavish and dead-heading is, as always, essential.

Certain plants here have been chosen for their exceptionally long flowering season. *Salvia neurepia*, the small scarlet sage, can be relied on for four months of the year and sometimes more. 'The Fairy' is a rose which starts late but then makes up for lost time by keeping going for three months on end, and the geranium is never without a clear pink flower throughout the summer months.

Penstemons and violas like a mid-season rest, when they need to be cut back. This allows them to gather their strength for another burst of flower late in the year. Although penstemons will survive mild winters, old plants seem to flower less well than young ones. Taking cuttings at the end of the season ensures an impressive supply of flowers for the following year, as well as avoiding the risk of losing plants in a hard winter.

A plant which is definitely not hardy is the verbena, and if the effort of growing it seems too much, one of the

Dianthus barbatus auricula-eyed

(sweet william)

Dianthus

'Brympton Red'

Rosa

'The Fairy'

diascias might stand a better chance.

It is an undeniable fact, though, that intense displays of colour cannot do without a few annuals and biennials to keep them going. Modern gardeners who work on small canvases are particularly dependent on ephemeral plants if they want a constant display of colour. Labour-saving shrubs were invented for public spaces and large gardens when gardeners' wages had ceased to be affordable and low maintenance gardens became desirable. The carpet-bedding and 'mosaiculture' that were the mainstay of Victorian gardening relied on the availability of virtually unlimited colourful annuals and cheap labour. Do-it-yourself gardeners can afford to indulge in special effects like these only because their space is small enough not to be too demanding.

Rosa

'Ferdinand Pichard'

Paeonia officinalis

'Rubra Plena' (peony)

Lilium regale

(regal lily)

Penstemon

'Garnet'

Purple with White

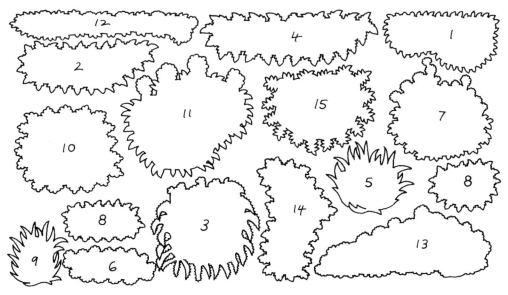

Suggested underplanting throughout: *Tulipa* 'Queen of Night', *T.* 'Shirley', *Crocus sieberi* 'Bowles' White', *C. s.* 'Violet Queen', *Erythronium dens-canis* (dog's-tooth violet) and *Cyclamen coum*. Edging: *Buxus suffruticosa* (dwarf box)

Early

1 *Osmanthus delavayi* with *Lathyrus latifolius* (perennial pea/mid-late)

2 *Lunaria annua variegata alba* (white variegated honesty)

3 *Helleborus orientalis orientalis*, syn. *H. o. olympicus* (lenten rose)

Early-mid

4 *Abutilon* x *suntense* or *Clematis* x *jackmanii* or *C. viticella* 'Etoile Violette'

5 *Iris graminea* (plum tart iris)

6 *Saxifraga* x *urbium* (London pride)

Mid

7 *Thalictrum aquilegifolium* 'White Cloud' (meadow rue)

8 *Viola* 'Huntercombe Purple'

9 *Iris pallida* 'Variegata'

10 *Rosa nutkana* 'Plena', syn. *R. californica* 'Plena'

11 *Phlox maculata* 'Omega'

Mid-late

12 *Solanum jasminoides* 'Album' or *Rosa* 'Mme Alfred Carrière'

13 *Epilobium glabellum* (willow-herb)

14 *Geranium* 'Russell Prichard'

15 *Hebe* 'La Séduisante'

*T*his sophisticated purple and white mix might look better in a town garden against a white-painted trellis or a whitewashed wall than surrounded by green in a country garden. A nucleus of winter interest (which is especially important in an urban setting) is provided by the group of osmanthus, hebe and hellebore, and around these early crocus fill the gaps left when herbaceous perennials die back in winter.

Under the rose more bulbs could be added (there is always room for more bulbs to provide a layer of extra interest in every flowerbed). The dog's-tooth violet, which likes shade and moist rich conditions, can also sometimes be persuaded to share the lot of a rose, but on very dry soil cyclamen are safer.

In this design some provision for keeping the ground damp around the phlox would be sensible, and this might perhaps be extended to the rose and the viola. Phlox make miserable specimens on fast-draining soils in sun, but with modern perforated hoses which can be buried around specific plants they can now be placed almost anywhere. Technology like this means that the range of plants which can be grown on dry soil is no longer limited to those which, like camels, can survive desert conditions.

Plantsmen would probably wince at the idea of growing a hebe next to a phlox, as the requirements of these plants are so different. Hebes thrive in dry sandy places in the sun, while phlox like cool rich soil. But if well tended neither plant need suffer. If the phlox has its own irrigation system and plenty of mulch, both plants may be relied upon to perform well. It is only in the smallest gardens that it is possible to go to such lengths to create artificial microclimates for plants, but it is worth manipulating nature – in fact it is

for only part of the day. A *Clematis × jackmanii* or *C. viticella* 'Etoile Violette' might replace the abutilon, and another rose, the white 'Mme Alfred Carrière', could be substituted for the solanum. These would admittedly be less distinguished than the original pair, but they would keep the same combination of colours going.

Because this is a sharp and sophisticated planting it might be improved by a note of formality. Edging a bed all the way round with one plant, in this case perhaps the geranium or the London pride, can change the way you look at it. Adding another clump of variegated iris on the right to balance the one on the left might take this formality a stage further. This sort of treatment is not always an improvement, and where the arrangement of colours creates a misty haze it is lovely to maintain that illusion with irregular groups and drifts of plants. But where the contrast is as sharp as it is with these purple and white flowers, formalizing the arrangements and possibly giving them a touch of symmetry can give the bed an added sophistication.

■

unavoidable – if you are determined to combine certain colours and textures. I think the technical challenge of growing exactly what you want where you want it gives gardening an extra dimension. It is after all no more unnatural to do this than to grow a plant in a pot, which is something that even the most 'natural' of gardeners cannot resist.

Abutilons and solanums need warm walls, and should then flower for months, but if these were changed to a couple of climbers which will tolerate shade, the rest of the border could manage with an aspect that was in sun

Epilobium glabellum

(willow-herb)

Purple and white make a smart combination. Although the hebe may not always survive the coldest of winters, in the protected microclimate of a city garden this sophisticated planting would always look fresh. (Early-mid)

Helleborus orientalis orientalis

(lenten rose)

Iris pallida

'Variegata'

Solanum jasminoides

'Album'

Tulipa

'Queen of Night'

Rich Pink and Pale Pink

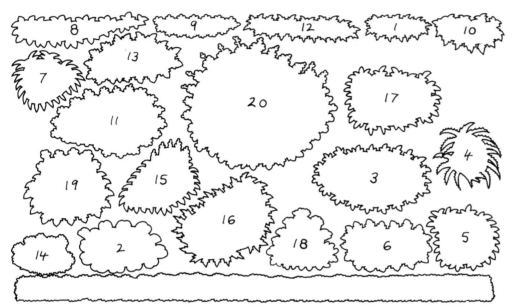

Suggested underplanting throughout: *Tulipa* 'Shirley', *T.* 'Angélique' and *Lilium regale*

Early

1 *Clematis montana* 'Elizabeth'
2 *Bergenia crassifolia*

Early-mid

3 *Daphne retusa*

Mid

4 *Morina longifolia* (whorl flower)
5 *Stachys byzantina*, syn. *S. olympica*
6 *Heuchera* 'Apple Blossom'
7 *Hesperis matronalis* (sweet rocket)
8 *Actinidia kolomikta*
9 *Rosa* 'Mme Grégoire Staechelin'
10 *Abutilon vitifolium* 'Veronica Tennant'
11 *Rosa* 'De Rescht'

Mid-late

12 *Clematis* 'Kermesina', syn. *C.* 'Viticella Rubra'
13 *Anemone hupehensis japonica* 'Prinz Heinrich' (Japanese anemone)
14 *Diascia vigilis*
15 *Penstemon* 'Garnet'
16 *Potentilla nepalensis* 'Miss Willmott' (cinquefoil)
17 *Salvia involucrata* 'Bethellii'

Late

18 *Sedum spectabile* (ice plant)
19 *Cosmos atrosanguineus*
20 *Lavatera olbia* 'Barnsley' (tree mallow)

Rich pinks provide a burst of summer colour in this group intended for a place in the sun. There is little here for the rest of the year, but plenty to see in the hot months.
(Mid-late)

A lavish summer border in a range of rich pinks and maroons needs sun for at least part of the day. It is interesting to compare this planting with the clear pink and crimson cottage collection, because although they appear to share a common colour base the results are very different. The cottage border looks fresh and lively, while this one has a heavier, drowsier feeling. Here there is more blue in the pinks and reds, which darkens the picture. Even the 'Barnsley' mallow, whose flowers are porcelain pale, has a shade of blue in it. Try putting it with some 'The Fairy' roses and you will see that in spite of the fact that both are pink and one – the mallow – is almost white, they do not improve one another.

The mallow, a comparatively new introduction, already risks becoming a garden cliché, for its three months in flower have earned it a place in gardens everywhere. However it does have one bad habit: in time it can revert to the old puce version of *Lavatera olbia*, the parent plant. Renewing the shrub from cuttings every two to three years is a sensible precaution. It is a fast grower and not difficult to root, so if it constantly throws up shoots with darker flowers you should have it out and replace it with a young scion.

No summer patch of flowers, however small, is complete without a rose. *Rosa* 'De Rescht' is an unusually neat shrub with velvet dark flowers which appear throughout the summer. Like many of the best plants it is not widely available, but for small gardens it has all the attractions of the old shrub roses with none of their disadvantages. The other rose chosen, 'Mme Grégoire Staechelin', sometimes called 'Spanish Beauty', flowers only once, but with such abundance and with so many double roses that you can forgive her for not putting in a second appearance. This one comes in singing pink, the sort that silences a crowd. Some colours are as heady as wine, and the pink of the Spanish Beauty is like a 'beaker full of the warm South'.

In a group of plants designed above all for colour-seekers, the shape of the flowers becomes secondary. The salvia is an interesting plant, but what you notice first about it is the shocking pink of its curious flowers. The penstemon, too, is before all else a patch of rich crimson, and the cosmos is remarkable for its maroon-black flowers. All these and the pink diascia are doubtfully hardy, but in light soil and a sunny place they can survive the winter – although they flower better if cuttings are taken in the autumn and kept under glass in the cold months.

Summer colour comes first in this group, which means that there is very little to attract interest over the rest of the year. The daphne makes an evergreen dome, however, and the morina, whose prickly whorls open pink, keeps its thistle leaves throughout the winter. Evergreens too, the sedum and the stachys should survive all but the most extreme conditions, when their greyish leaves are likely to turn soggy.

Lavatera olbia
'Barnsley'

Salvia involucrata
'Bethellii'

Clematis 'Kermesina'
(syn. *C.* 'Viticella Rubra')

GREENS, GREYS and WHITES

*G*REEN IS THE BACKDROP FOR THE GARDEN,
*but in its range of shades and textures
green has as much to offer as any foreground
interest. Grey dims, white brightens and greens,
greys and white together will outlast the flash
from coloured petals.*

*The famous White Garden at Sissinghurst
was probably more visited by Vita
Sackville-West at dusk and under the moon
than in the light of day. This mixture of
silvery leaves and bracts with white flowers
and green leaves would look even more
dramatic by moonlight than in sunshine.*

The large Euphorbia wulfenii *is one of the best 'green on green' plants. A gold-splashed ivy as a companion completes the picture.*

'Although I like white on white, the major push is for green on green,' writes Robert Dash, the American artist whose Long Island garden is respected for its subtlety. As a painter he confesses a predilection for 'shape, mass and form', having 'learned that the predominate colour of gardens is green and all the rest rather secondary bedeckment.' This sounds austere but he is right. Gardens in a limited or even monochromatic range of colours have much to offer. 'Meanwhile the mind, from pleasure less, withdraws into its happiness . . . Annihilating all that's made to a green thought in a green shade,' wrote the seventeenth-century poet Andrew Marvell in his poem 'The Garden'. His lines express better than any others that I know the power of green, which can blot out everything else in the garden. Green's properties of shade and coolness sometimes make the 'push for green on green' irresistible. In towns, particularly, the colour of grass and trees reminds people imprisoned by pavements of what

Green inevitably predominates in the garden, but it need not be dull: there can be many variations of shade as well as different leaf shapes. Here narrow grasses and finely cut blue rue make interesting changes of texture and tone.

they have lost. In hot places, the green of hedges and leaves of trees without any flowers are enough to suggest a garden, especially if the sound of water can be heard. Around any building green softens hard lines and links the man-made world with the natural one, making a bridge into the landscape. And where a view extends beyond the garden to the surrounding countryside bright beds of flowers are often inappropriate. Green plants can smooth the transition from garden to field without breaking the spell of the view.

The predominance of green in any garden is inevitable, but should not be dull. A craving for variety can be satisfied with no flowers at all, provided that there are not too many small oval leaves of shrubs like privet, forsythia or lilac. Featureless plants like these look less than refreshing when out of season, so green on green compositions must rely on texture and shape for their effect. Most of the so-called architectural plants, the ones which

Green and white make a refreshing group in any garden, particularly in an urban setting. The white agapanthus is less often seen than the blue one, but is well worth seeking out. White flowers are always useful for lighting dark corners.

make you stop and look, and which provide great punctuation marks in a garden, are green. Think of acanthus, melianthus, bergenia, fennel, fatsia, euphorbia, upright juniper and rosemary, to name but a few. All these different species with their variously shaped leaves add interest and changes of scale or emphasis to the garden. If flowers can be classified as 'secondary bedeckment', leaves must surely qualify for the title of primary decoration.

Ephemeral and chancy, flowers are endearing because they are so elusive. Leaves are much more dependable, and if a garden looks good when out of flower, colour can only become a bonus. Green, it has to be admitted, is much the easiest colour to handle out of doors. There is so much of it about that beating it into submission is hard work, so you might as well join it occasionally (a heavy hand with the coloured foliage, which some see as a way of subduing green, is not I think the best tactic). Subtly handled, green can be as effective an ally as any of the other colours which wash the senses with waves of varying moods; and where most colours can do little more than rearrange the spirits or assault the eye, green has the extra advantage of adding texture to a planting, as well as suggesting all sorts of qualities that flowers can never convey. Green can always be relied upon to freshen the soul and produce a sense of peace. But chlorophyll can do more than this: green plants may suggest by turn that they are exotic, airy, neat, cheerful or mature. Try attaching all those qualities to a red or blue flower and you will appreciate the versatility of nature's favourite colour. Consider the exoticism of the large leaves of melianthus or fatsia, or of the finely-cut airiness of robinia or fennel, which can lighten any planting. Then imagine the dark of large clipped evergreens, which give a garden a settled, mature look, or think of smaller hedges of box, thyme or parsley, which convey a sense of order. Some greens can even be cheerful: when the glossy leaves of plants like holly or Portugal laurel (*Prunus lusitanica*) catch the light, they brighten dull corners. Few other colours offer so much value and variety.

Compare the effect of hostas in a variety of greens, which stimulate the eye, with the restful quality of the single blue form opposite.

Gertrude Jekyll liked to say that green gardens were best left for large-scale settings, but Margery Fish, the cottage gardener of the 1950s, popularized green flowers and foliage for small gardens, showing that green was not just for parks and grass. She had a green garden where she grew such curiosities as the green rose (*R. chinensis* 'Viridiflora') and the astrantia 'Shaggy' which is often associated with her name. The influence of Margery Fish was an important one for small gardens. The rich patterns of leaves in different shades of green paling to silver that were adopted by Mrs

The white rambler roses 'The Garland' and 'Kiftsgate', with the pink-tinged 'Francis E. Lester', have a short season but a lovely one. Notice the silvery buds of the senecio below, just before they break into bright yellow daisies.

This single white tree peony under a Cornus florida *makes an unforgettable spring picture. It may look rather forlorn later, so is not for the small garden.*

Opposite: White wisteria is another ephemeral delight, but it may be worth sacrificing all-year interest for a display like this.

In this planting it is interesting to compare the different effects made by the solid silver group of Senecio maritima, *with the broken white of the airy gypsophila behind, and the dense clump of white phlox at the back of the group.*

Fish were then used less flamboyantly than is now the rule. Silver plants are, I think, sometimes overdone in today's plantings. Their metallic quality can make too stark a contrast with other plants; silver leaves, like white flowers, draw the eye, but unlike white flowers they are not ephemeral. Plants like *Artemisia* 'Powis Castle' or *Senecio* 'Sunshine', for example, become fixtures in a changing border. They can end up looking like solid pewter lumps among filmy green leaves and bright evanescent petals. People rely on greys to 'tone down' a planting, but these are not natural background features, and they often have the reverse effect, tending instead to smarten and brighten up the very group of plants that they were sent to subdue.

Dim and bright greys have very different effects. Imagine for instance a group of deep pink roses surrounded by *Artemisia* 'Powis Castle'. This combination would make quite a strong picture, whereas if the grey were the softer shade of old-fashioned lavender (*L. angustifolia*) the association of pink and grey would be much gentler on the eye. Grey foliage is lovely, but it needs careful handling.

White flowers are easier to place, and have become the fall-back of many modern gardeners. Their inspiration is the White Garden at Sissinghurst, where Vita Sackville-West 'could not help hoping that the great ghostly barn owl will sweep silently across a pale garden, next summer, in the twilight, the pale garden that I am now planting, under the first flakes of snow.' The mood of this garden was perhaps more one of night than of white, for Vita Sackville-West was obliged to walk through her garden every evening, as she worked, slept and ate in three separate buildings. The pale twilight garden of willow-leaved pear tree, silvery artemisias, regale lilies, delphiniums, roses, silver buckthorns, foxgloves, tree peonies and numberless other white plants must have had a magical quality about it that the visitor to Sissinghurst by day never sees. In sunlight the White Garden becomes a much smarter affair, and it is this daytime version which has been copied and diminished by so many of her disciples. 'Iceberg' roses, a few ivory foxgloves and some santolina at midday are a travesty of their moonlit original. But, secure in the knowledge that white flowers will offend no one and will lend equal grace to brick, stone, timber or any other material, 'discerning' gardeners continue to choose white as their favourite colour.

Green and White

Suggested underplanting throughout: *Tulipa* 'Spring Green'

Early

1 *Helleborus lividus corsicus* (hellebore)
2 *Clematis cirrhosa balearica*

Early-mid

3 *Prunus laurocerasus* 'Otto Luyken'
(cherry laurel)
4 *Choisya ternata* (Mexican orange
blossom)

Mid

5 *Angelica archangelica*
6 *Digitalis purpurea alba* (white foxglove)
underplanted with *Tulipa* 'White
Triumphator' (early)
7 *Hosta sieboldiana*

Mid-late

8 *Clematis* x *jouiniana* 'Praecox'
9 *Rosa* 'Mme Alfred Carrière'
10 *Astrantia major* (masterwort)
11 *Rosa* 'Yvonne Rabier'
12 *Bupleurum fruticosum*
(shrubby hare's ear)
13 *Acanthus spinosus*
14 *Polystichum setiferum*
(soft shield fern)
15 *Nicotiana langsdorfii*
(tobacco plant)

*G*reen and white plants present a particularly effective combination in shady places. This collection contains the blue-green leaves of hosta and bupleurum, but no silvers. It makes a cool group in summer and a cheerful one in winter, with glossy evergreens and a few late winter green flowers on the Balearic clematis.

It is a feature of white flowers on open sites that they become luminous towards nightfall. But in dark corners, where light is lower, white petals shine out from gloomy recesses all day long. Glossy leaves also help to reflect what light there is (which is why they look so cheerful in winter), so the choisya and 'Otto Luyken' laurel are a good choice as much for their shiny evergreen leaves as for their white flowers.

There is always a risk that roses will under-perform in semi-shade, but 'Mme Alfred Carrière' is less fussy than most about sun. Climbing roses tend to grow better in shade than bush ones and 'Yvonne Rabier' might sulk too badly to warrant a place here if the aspect were very poor. If so a white-flowering *Chaenomeles speciosa*, or japonica, would be a promising substitute, although there is the disadvantage that it would not provide summer flowers. Japonicas are underrated shrubs, being easy to grow if a little slow to flower in their infancy. Any new growth needs heavy pruning, as they flower on old wood.

Bupleurum, which colonizes Mediterranean hills, is also obliging in cooler climates, often enjoying itself so much that it grows too big for its allocated space. It could, in time, fill the whole of the area shown if it were unchecked by severe winters and never pruned, but it is worth trying to keep it within bounds for this scheme, as its leaves are lovely all year and the yellow-green late summer flowers are a magnet for hoverflies.

The flowers of the bupleurum are nearer to yellow than green, but there

Tulipa

'White Triumphator'

are others which are closer to lime. Angelica is not often grown by less than enthusiastic gardeners who avoid plants which need frequent renewal, but this huge herb does nevertheless seed itself – not always where you want it, of course, but seedlings can be transplanted at the end of their first year, and the following season will make a six-foot-tall spectacle of cloudy green. Preventing the plant from setting seed can sometimes keep it going for another year, but on the whole it is easier to treat angelica as a biennial.

Nicotiana langsdorfii is the only other plant here which uncommitted gardeners might want to avoid, but it is such a delicate thing with its pale green flower bells that it is worth the trouble of finding it or growing it each season. In warm gardens it should survive the winter. Many of the plans in this collection rely on plants like the nicotiana which are a little unusual but not difficult to grow. *Clematis* × *jouiniana* is unlikely to be found in

A shady corner would suit this cheerful collection for winter, which includes plenty of evergreens with glossy leaves. In summer cool greens and white flowers are grouped round the unusual bupleurum at the centre of the bed. (Mid-late)

every nursery, but it is pretty, spreading trails of watery bluish-white flowers into its neighbours late in the summer. When the foxgloves are over and while the choisya rests, the clematis should fill the place of the first and climb all over the second. 'Praecox' is the form to seek here, as it flowers earlier in the season than the unnamed variety.

After the initial labour involved in tracking down unusual plants, this group should be one of the easiest to manage of all the plans in this book. Agreeable rather than spectacular, it ought to furnish an unpromising corner with something of interest for much of the year.

■

Acanthus spinosus

(bear's breeches)

Helleborus lividus corsicus

(hellebore)

PLAN: GREEN and WHITE 73

Green on Green

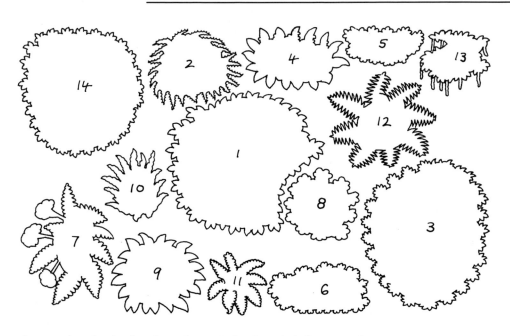

Suggested underplanting throughout: *Galanthus* 'Ophelia' (snowdrop), *G.* 'Desdemona', *G. elwesii* and *Leucojum aestivum* 'Gravetye Giant' (snowflake)

Very early

1 *Viburnum tinus* 'Eve Price'

Early

2 *Helleborus foetidus* 'Wester Flisk' or Miss Jekyll's scented form
3 *Sarcococca hookeriana digyna* (Christmas box)

Early-mid

4 *Convallaria majalis* (lily of the valley)
5 *Lonicera japonica* 'Halliana' (honeysuckle)
6 *Saxifraga* x *urbium* (London pride)
7 *Myrrhis odorata* (sweet cicely)

Mid

8 *Alchemilla mollis* (lady's mantle)
9 *Hosta plantaginea* (August lily)
10 *Phyllitis scolopendrium*, syn. *Asplenium scolopendrium* (hart's-tongue fern)
11 *Polystichum setiferum* (soft shield fern)
12 *Dryopteris filix-mas* (male fern)

Mid-late

13 *Itea ilicifolia*
14 *Ligustrum lucidum* (Chinese privet)

A winter bed below a window can provide a green picture all through the year. This group of plants would grow on the shady side of the house and includes several scented flowers to sniff on warmer days. The Christmas box has spidery threads of flower, unobtrusive but they smell delicious. Lilies of the valley, which need no introduction, will survive in a forgotten dark corner for years but are improved by an annual helping of leaf-mould. The evergreen honeysuckle, sweet cicely (which should not be allowed to seed) and even the Chinese privet are all scented.

So too is the *Hosta plantaginea*, whose fragrant white flowers open on summer evenings. This is a hosta which prefers sunny conditions, but will tolerate some shade. The Miss Jekyll's scented form of the common *Helleborus foetidus* is sadly hard to find; there are other sweet-smelling 'stinking hellebores', but in their absence it might be better to opt for the variety *H.* 'Wester Flisk', or the dependable *Helleborus corsicus*.

The central feature of the bed is a clipped dome of the familiar *Viburnum tinus* in its best form: 'Eve Price' has pink-tinged flowers which open to a clean white, and the leaves of this modest grower are a good dark green. A large-leaved bush like this needs careful clipping: it spoils the effect if the leaves are snipped in half by shears, so it is worth tidying up the damaged ones with a pair of secateurs at the end of the operation.

The other dominating shrubs are the elegant Chinese privet, which will make a self-supporting tree if left to itself, and is therefore a good plant to stand against a house wall if you want to minimize the work of tying and training. The itea, similarly obliging, is

not unlike a *Garrya elliptica* in appearance, with long tassel flowers which appear in autumn. Here it is preferable because of its shiny leaves, less gloomy than the matt foliage of the garrya; but the garrya's outsize catkins come early in the year when few flowers are out, which might sway some gardeners in its favour.

Ferns fill several of the spaces between plants, because their beautiful shapes are interesting virtually all the year. It is a popular misconception that they need damp places to survive; they do, however, prefer a crumbly open soil. Any leaf-mould left over from the lilies of the valley will suit them well, and in very dry springs extra watering

A green and white composition of hostas, ferns, alchemilla, euphorbia and white valerian. Without the white window frame it would look less fresh.

Myrrhis odorata

(sweet cicely)

Phyllitis scolopendrium

(hart's-tongue fern)

can help them to face the summer: they seem to be able to manage on less water once they have reached their full size. The hart's-tongue fern is reliably evergreen and the other two should keep their leaves for the first half of the winter. In mild years they will probably all stay green.

Because it is near the house a bed like this should receive plenty of attention, which makes it a good site for a collection of named large snowdrops: only close inspection will reveal their markings and their pure white bells are well set off by a background of different greens. But if the idea of an all-green bed with no white flowers appeals, more hellebores or fritillaries (*F. pyrenaica* or *F. pontica*) would provide green flowers. Fritillaries are temperamental and like well-drained deep soils, so they would not be everyone's choice. Less patient gardeners might like to put green tobacco plants, *Nicotiana alata* 'Lime Green', into any gaps for summer. The arrangement here provides no summer spectacle, only a quiet tapestry of leaves in all shades of green.

Convallaria majalis

(lily of the valley)

Itea ilicifolia

■

Helleborus foetidus

'Wester Flisk'

Silver and White

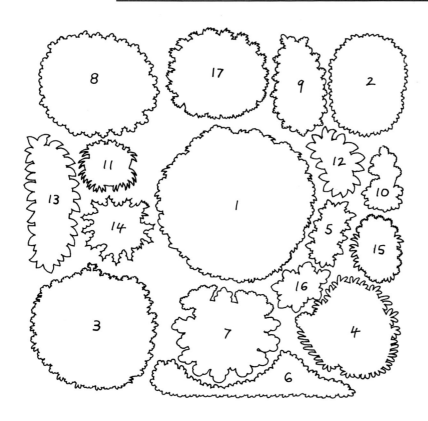

Suggested underplanting throughout: *Tulipa* 'Purissima', *Lilium candidum* (madonna lily), *L. regale* (regal lily) and *Centranthus ruber albus* (white valerian)

Early
1 *Magnolia salicifolia* or *Pyrus calleryana* 'Chanticleer'
2 *Sarcococca hookeriana digyna* (Christmas box)
3 *Olearia x scilloniensis*
4 *Euphorbia characias wulfenii* (spurge)

Early-mid
5 *Lunaria annua variegata alba* (white variegated honesty)
6 *Viola cornuta alba*

Mid
7 *Crambe maritima* (sea kale)
8 *Rosa* 'Dupontii' (snowbush rose)
9 *Lysimachia ephemerum* (loosestrife)
10 *Filipendula vulgaris* 'Plena', syn. *F. hexapetala* 'Flore Pleno' (dropwort)
11 *Campanula lactiflora alba*
12 *Digitalis purpurea alba* (white foxglove)
13 *Hosta fortunei* 'Marginata Alba'
14 *Onopordum acanthium* (Scotch thistle) or *Silybum marianum* (milk thistle)

Mid-late
15 *Anaphalis triplinervis* (pearl everlasting)
16 *Alcea rosea* single white, syn. *Althaea rosea* (single white hollyhock)
17 *Artemisia* 'Powis Castle'

The obvious choice for the centre of this silver and white arrangement would have been a weeping silver-leaved pear. However this small tree has been the first resort of so many for so long that if you want to create a more unusual and fresh-looking effect you need to search for something less hackneyed. The willow-leaved magnolia does have greyish-white leaves and a neat conical shape, but it is its large scented flowers in spring and the faintly aromatic quality of its leaves that make it an interesting substitute for the pear.

The other choice here might have been the less well-known pear 'Chanticleer', which is covered with blossom in spring but has green leaves. Fruit blossom, and especially pear blossom, is one of the most beautiful sights of spring. It seems a pity not to include it in every garden.

There will one day be no room to plant around whatever tree you choose, but until that happens, and while the tree is too small to stand on its own, there will be the added fun of these complementary plants at its feet.

This bed is designed to be walked round, and has a strong plant placed to emphasize each corner. The euphorbia and the sarcococca, which bears small fragrant flowers at the time of year when there is not much else in the garden, are for enjoying in winter and

Crambe maritima

(sea kale)

Anaphalis triplinervis

(pearl everlasting)

Campanula lactiflora alba

■

early spring; progressing round the bed, the euphorbia can also be admired later with the daisy-studded olearia. Then, following the olearia, the rose comes into its own. This is a greyish bush which bears single white flowers like large wild roses. When these are over the artemisia and hosta should make up for the rose's lack-lustre leaves.

The artemisia is often asked to play a subordinate role in planting schemes, but here it is a feature in its own right because silver is all important. In a plan which relies on whitish-grey leaves for its effect it may be felt that the silver quotient in the rose's leaves will not make a significant enough contribution in this respect.

If you want to capitalize on silver, *Senecio* 'Sunshine' is worth considering as an alternative, provided you can bear to lose the roses. The yellow daisies which appear on the senecio are no compensation for the lack of flowers: they are a difficult adornment at the best of times, and here would sully the arrangement altogether, so purists

Opposite: Onopordum acanthium *with white foxgloves. This large and statuesque thistle needs cutting down after flowering, but its seed should be saved.*

Clotted-cream foxgloves above silvery artemisias will not last long, but together they make a lovely if ephemeral midsummer image.

would live-head the silvery buds as they begin to open. Such ruthlessness may seem unnatural, but if you think about it is no worse than cutting grass or hedges. Gardens are after all by definition cultivated and unnatural places.

Some of the other silver plants will need a little attention to keep them going. The thistles (onopordum and silybum) and honesty are all biennials but should seed themselves with a little encouragement. They will all earn their place for months so it is worth the effort of growing them.

The sea kale is not a passenger plant either. Its crinkled blue-grey leaves make a strong foil for other plants and last long after the honey-scented flowers have faded. If the flower heads are cut down and any withered leaves

picked off, this plant will go on being an eyecatching feature throughout the summer months.

The tall plants are inevitably foxgloves, lysimachia and campanulas, as they are in many other designs in this book. Hollyhocks in single forms also break the line of rounded plants, but will need renewing every year if rust is to be avoided. Lilies are also good accent plants where space is short, but in some places the advent of the lily beetle has made them troublesome to grow. The madonna lily is often temperamental, but regales, which are easy to raise from seed, can generally be kept going in all but the driest of gardens. In late summer this patch of ethereal silvery leaves with white flowers would definitely be one to enjoy on moonlit evenings.

Centranthus ruber albus

(white valerian)

YELLOWS

*G*OLD AND YELLOW ARE THE LIGHT-
bringers, which draw the eye to
their own radiance. Luminous and weightless, a
scattering of pale yellow flowers gives an airy
feeling to any group. But, responsive as they are
to light, yellows need careful placing.

*Yellow and gold flowers give the impression
of a burst of sunshine on grey days, but they
need to be used with caution as they can
look brassy when the sun comes out.*

The golden haloes of saints in early Christian art symbolized their transfiguration into a realm of light. So gold and yellow suggest sun and glory, for they are the light-bringers which draw the eye, shining out from other shades like a more substantial form of white. Yellow brightens and cheers with its associations of spring sunshine and daffodils, or of hot harvests and ripe corn. But although a dark corner can be illuminated by a patch of gold, yellow can also have more complex associations than sunshine and primroses. Think of moonlight, which is silver-yellow not gold, or of the sear and yellow leaves of autumn, which suggest a very different mood. It can be a melancholy colour and a cold one: not for nothing was Judas painted by Holbein and Giotto in sad yellow. Think too of wasps in their armour of black and yellow, a combination of the darkest and the brightest which turns yellow into a vicious colour.

Yellow shares with blue a dual nature, inducing either happy moods or sad ones. The major and minor keys of blue and yellow are more sharply defined than those of other colours. What is more, although yellow appears to be the most lovable shade in the gardener's paint box, it is in fact one of the hardest to use. Blue cannot always be relied upon to produce a feeling of well-being, but it is rarely disagreeable in a garden setting. Yellow can be horrible. The chief reason for this is the changing quality of light in the garden, which affects yellow more than any other colour. Under the watery suns of spring yellows appear clear and fresh, but bright summer sunlight turns all the gold to brass. For brassiness is a charge which it is easy to level at yellow summer borders, where golden rod and sunflowers blaze back at an August sun. Then later in the year, as the light loses its brilliance, yellow becomes acceptable again, and the muted sunlight of autumn afternoons mellows golden leaves or flowers.

Pale yellow tree lupins and the silver-grey leaves of Jerusalem sage make a balanced counter-point to the sombre blue-greens of Euphorbia wulfenii and the new greens of wisteria and abutilon.

Candelabra primulas, which like shady damp places, make a lovely spring feature near water.

Gertrude Jekyll wrote that she had always wanted a gold garden: she planned, but never planted, a hedged enclosure where permanent shrubs would look bright and cheerful all year round. At Crathes Castle in Scotland there is such a planting which was largely inspired by her plans. I doubt though whether many small gardens could afford the room for this sort of effect, for although it would be cheerful enough on grey days, on sunny ones it would have a relentless quality which would exhaust the eye. The garden at Crathes has enough different areas to allow the visitor a choice of places to go on hot days, but on a smaller scale the effect would be rather similar to lighting a fire outside at midday in summer. Flames fascinate at night or when it is cold and grey, but they can look almost synthetic in the heat of the day. Gold plantings look similarly tawdry under the sun, and flowers as well as shrubs in predominantly yellow shades are perhaps best avoided in places where the sun's rays strike hardest. But yellow need not be denied to modern gardeners: used with care, it can highlight any planting. I can think of no colour scheme to which it would be

The perennial sage (Phlomis russeliana), like the primula, has a habit of arranging its flowers in tiers and prefers dry sunny places.

Opposite: Yellow Lysimachia punctata brightens and defines the blues of hosta leaves and Jacob's ladder (Polemonium caeruleum).

A sunset group from
Sissinghurst, of mixed
blood-red wallflowers
under the early pale
yellow species Rosa
hugonis *with the*
evanescent Paeonia
mlokosewitschii,
makes an unusual
spring colour scheme.

difficult to introduce a shaft of lemon yellow, and provided it is
planted in a shady spot, you can even enjoy a Jekyll-inspired
golden afternoon every day of the year.

Yellow among sunset colours makes a strong picture, which can
be made to work on a small scale. The Cottage Garden at
Sissinghurst has yellow-leaved plants such as *Helichrysum*
petiolatum growing among gold pansies, day lilies, achilleas and
sunflowers. Here scarlet and orange flowers like dahlias,
nasturtiums, lilies and snapdragons are used to give life and
strength to the yellows. The garden is surrounded by golden
shrubs, but the orange and red flowers dominate and enrich the

Dazzling orange crocosmia and sulphurous achillea, growing together at Barnsley House, make a warm and daring colour combination, easier on the eye under the gentler sun of late summer than it would be earlier in the year.

mixture, keeping the yellows alive when the sun shines. These hot sunset colours need careful handling in small patches, but I think it is possible to stage-manage them if plenty of annuals (or half-hardy perennials) are used to keep the colours up to full strength all the time. Because it contains yellow, too much green will dilute the effect. This is not something to attempt either with plants which flower at a gentle pace. The aim is to saturate the place with colour, keeping the reds and oranges up to the strength of the yellows and occasionally even stronger.

In sunshine green leaves tend more to yellow than to blue, which can increase the amount of yellow in a planting to an unacceptable level. In shade, however, they are tinged with violet, which gives some relief to the eye in a yellow colour scheme. It is a garden cliché that yellow and purple suit one another perfectly (in fact they look hideous in strong measures), but there is some truth in this tradition. In dark corners, yellow is improved by the shadows which surround green leaves, which impart to them a hint of the purple that you will see if you stare and stare at yellow and then close your eyes. Besides, a shadowy dilution of violet with full-strength yellow seems much more appealing than the legacy of Victorian colour theorists, which gives us equal

The potentially harsh contrast between scarlet Lychnis chalcedonica and gold achillea is bridged here by a band of red-hot pokers, which contain both colours in paler measures.

The yellow rose 'Lawrence Johnston' with blue Ceanothus impressus *makes a composition that is both balanced and strong. Combinations of complementary colours have been popular with artists and designers since Monet's time and earlier. Lanning Roper was also particularly fond of using yellow and blue flowers in this way.*

quantities of purple and gold, a combination which always seems to me both hard and overbearing whether in sun or shade. It sometimes works if the emphasis is on full-strength purple and the yellow is diluted to palest cream: a planting of the common *Rhododendron ponticum* with creamy *Rosa hugonis* and pinky-mauve dicentra can look agreeable. If the yellow rose were even a shade brighter, however, it might spoil the picture.

Monet liked to lighten his purple contrasts to pink ones, growing sunflowers with pink hollyhocks for instance, but this sort of bold mixture needs space, which is I fear true of many daring colour combinations. They are designed to be seen from afar, and if yellow is included they need to be very far and quite bright if other colours are to attract as much attention as the all-dominating gold. If you must have a bright border in a confined space in the glare of the sun, and if yellow happens to be your favourite colour, try to place it against a sympathetic background – a grey stone wall, a white-painted fence or a green beech hedge perhaps. Then mix your yellows with masses of blue and a little white. Where space is not a problem, the pink and yellow of

Yellow flowers against a background of green foliage can look suprisingly sombre, depending on the shade of the leaves. Here the centaurea flowers have a tendency to look dull against the mid-green leaves, while the more solid yellow of the achillea, which has leaves that tend towards bluish silver, is easier on the eye.

Hemerocallis lilio-asphodelus, the scented day lily, is less showy than some of the modern hybrids, but its cool lemon-yellow flowers make a lovely contribution to any border. Pale yellows tend to be easier to place in modern gardens than hot golds.

winter jasmine, combined with the bright cerise *Salvia* 'Bethellii', nerines, late pale pink roses and a bush of golden privet can form the basis of a lively late autumn border, though this is a planting which will be at its best only in a mild autumn.

On a small scale there can be no doubt that the subtle approach works better. Van Gogh admired the intimate domestic pictures of the Dutch painter Jan Vermeer, singling out one portrait in a restricted palette of dull blue, lemon yellow, pearl grey, black and white. Without the black, for which green must double, this combination of colours can make a restful composition in the garden which will last for most of the year.

Used as an accent the light touch of yellow is invaluable. Vertical plants like foxgloves, mulleins and delphiniums add height and depth to any planting. In yellow or creamy white they lighten a border in both senses of the word, for yellow flowers, unlike red or blue ones, are weightless as well as luminous. An airy scattering of white flowers will freshen and co-ordinate an assortment of colours, but the same treatment with lemon yellow instead of white will look softer and more ethereal. The large

The rose here attracts all the attention because the pinky white flowers of the kolkwitzia are not strong enough to balance its clear yellow. A stronger pink would make a more equal partner for the rather over-bearing qualities of some yellows. Monet loved pink with yellow.

woolly mullein, the single yellow hollyhock or the pale form of evening primrose will all lighten even the stodgiest of plantings.

White is a good companion for yellow, because it seems to compensate for the extra yellow which goes into the making of green. Yellow on green is radiant and can (especially in sunlight) be too much of a good thing, but it is both subdued and clarified by white. So variegated plants with white- or cream-splashed leaves are helpful additions to yellow borders.

The instant impact of yellow makes it many gardeners' first choice. Daffodils and forsythia crowd other colours out of English spring gardens, but their easy brilliance ends up by spoiling their effect. For this reason, perhaps, more thoughtful gardeners avoid using too much yellow. It is harder to fit into the garden picture than pink or blue, but for those who are prepared to rise to the challenge, the support of yellow can light up as well as lighten the garden.

Opposite: Late summer borders like this one at Gunby Hall in Lincolnshire often look forward to the colours of autumn leaves with their range of warm bronzes and yellows, ochres and oranges.

A spring choice for a yellow-based border, with the acid lime bottlebrushes of the large euphorbia and chrome-yellow alyssum, makes a combination which would look very hard later in the year. In spring, however, the slanting sunlight waters down even sharp colours.

Pale Yellow and Grey

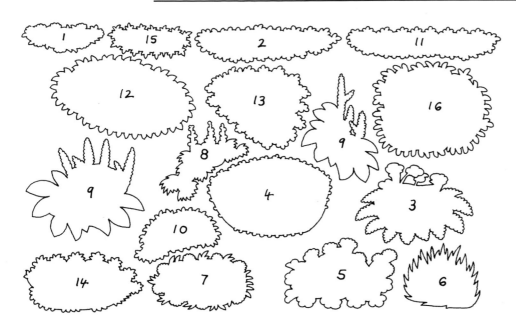

Suggested underplanting throughout: *Narcissus* 'February Silver', *Tulipa sylvestris*, *T.* 'Texas Gold' (yellow parrot) and *Oenothera tetragona* (evening primrose)

Early

1 *Jasminum nudiflorum* (winter-flowering jasmine)

Mid

2 *Lonicera periclymenum* 'Graham Thomas' (honeysuckle)

3 *Achillea* 'Moonshine' (yarrow)

4 *Santolina pinnata neapolitana*

5 *Alchemilla mollis* (lady's mantle)

6 *Sisyrinchium striatum*

7 *Cheiranthus cheiri* 'Moonlight' (wallflower)

8 *Aconitum vulparia* (monkshood)

9 *Verbascum olympicum* (mullein)

10 *Viola* 'Aspasia' or *V. cornuta alba*

Mid-late

11 *Rosa* 'Mermaid'

12 *Phygelius aequalis* 'Yellow Trumpet'

13 *Rosa* 'Golden Wings'

14 *Origanum vulgare aureum* (golden marjoram)

Late

15 *Clematis rehderiana*

16 *Elaeagnus* x *ebbingei* 'Limelight'

The second-best wall of a house (which is usually the one that gets half a day of declining sun) or any partly shaded place on a fence or garden wall, would be an ideal spot for this yellow and grey all-year group. Unlike the yellow and blue corner this is not designed to be at its best in the summer months, but to be enjoyed for most of the year. It will never look very flowery, although because there is plenty of static unchanging colour from the elaeagnus, it will never look dull. Work too will be less than it is in plantings where flower colour is maximized. The mood is cheerful in winter and quiet and cool, airy and elegant in the summer months.

Like shooting stars, the golden jasmine drops down the wall all winter and has a dramatic presence in the garden. Its companion through the hard weather is the elaeagnus, which bears silver, yellow and green leaves throughout the year. This variety is slower growing than the more usual variegated form, but worth the wait for its subtle patterning. The santolina too is an uncommon form with less silver leaves than the well-known cotton lavender, and with sulphur yellow flowers in summer rather than the usual bright gold. Like its relation it makes neat bushy shrubs of aromatic feathery foliage. All santolinas need a good haircut when the worst of the weather is past in order to keep them in shape for the summer months.

Even a subdued and unfloriferous planting can include a rose or two. 'Mermaid' is practically evergreen and its large single flowers appear all summer. It is a beast to prune, being thorny and vigorous, and it will probably become entangled with 'Graham Thomas', but I think it is worth climbing into a suit of armour twice a year to keep it within bounds. 'Golden Wings' is a more manageable affair; the advantage of both these roses

Clematis rehderiana

■

is that they do not demand to have sun on their faces.

Golden marjoram is another plant which can do without a suntan. Strong light affects its leaves, turning them brown, so this Mediterranean aromatic will be at its best in shade. Other plants which do not mind being deprived of sunshine are violas, which run about and climb into other plants so pleasingly, and the sinister monks-hood, which provides the always important vertical interest (although this form is inclined to lean).

The best verticals are the woolly grey verbascums, which would certainly prefer a place in full sun and well-drained soil, but it is worth trying them here for the sake of the picture. Plantsmen disapprove of manipulating

Mulleins like branching candelabra dominate this pale yellow and grey border for a warm wall. They are biennials but should self-seed. This is a low-key planting which is designed to look good all through the year. (Mid)

plants in this way in order to make them grow in places which they would not naturally choose, but a garden is a work of artifice – otherwise it would be a field – so I like breaking the rules occasionally.

If the verbascums fail and your site is very shady you can always revert to the book. Foxgloves would be an obvious substitute for them, especially the creamy yellow form *Digitalis lutea*, although they lack the grey velvety leaves which are such a desirable

feature of the Greek verbascum.

The phygelius needs a sheltered place, but in my experience it too can manage without direct sun. This is evergreen in good winters, with a long season of elegant creamy yellow tubular flowers which will last well into the autumn. It is the sort of plant which you will very probably not notice from afar, but which is interesting at close quarters. The same is true of many of the plants on this plan. A collection which is easy to live with like this one will not impress or surprise, but will make a balanced and agreeable part of the garden which you should be able to enjoy on most days of the year.

■

Pale Yellow and Blue

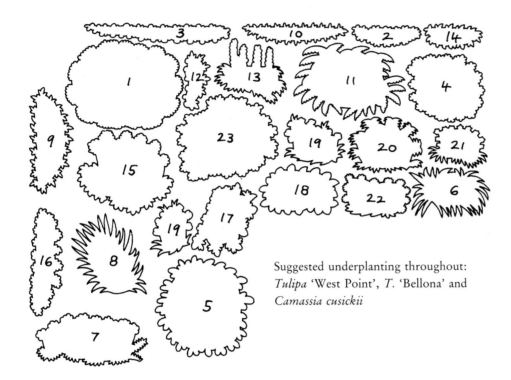

Early
1 *Acacia dealbata* (mimosa)
2 *Azara microphylla* (vanilla)

Early-mid
3 *Ceanothus* 'Cascade'
4 *Rosa hugonis*
5 *Paeonia mlokosewitschii* (peony)
6 *Hemerocallis lilio-asphodelus*, syn.
   H. flava (day lily)

Mid
7 *Polemonium caeruleum* (Jacob's ladder)
8 *Iris sibirica* 'Splash Down'
9 *Clematis* 'Perle d'Azur'
10 *Clematis* 'Mrs Cholmondeley'
11 *Melianthus major* (honey bush)
12 *Cephalaria gigantea* (giant scabious)
13 *Delphinium* Belladonna 'Wendy'

Mid-late
14 *Clematis orientalis* 'Sherriffii'
15 *Thalictrum flavum*
16 *Rosa* 'Alister Stella Gray'
17 *Geranium* 'Johnson's Blue'
   (crane's-bill)
18 *Salvia patens* 'Cambridge Blue'
19 *Oenothera tetragona*
   (evening primrose)
20 *Foeniculum vulgare* (fennel)
21 *Campanula persicifolia*
22 *Argyranthemum maderense*
23 *Rosa* 'Tynwald'

Suggested underplanting throughout:
Tulipa 'West Point', *T.* 'Bellona' and
Camassia cusickii

Groups of plants which aim to provide something to look at for much of the year often dilute their summer impact by carrying a dead-weight of evergreens at the back of the border. Where space is not short this can be camouflaged, but small gardens need winter shrubs which have a life after the cold months to form the backbone of a colour scheme. Bunches of the yellow bobbled flowers of mimosa are sold on winter streets, and its ferny leaves in bluish grey are lovely all year round. Mimosa is a borderline survivor, but in sheltered corners like this one it is often possible to grow plants which are marginally hardy. Many of these grow fast, so if they do succumb to a bad winter they can be replaced without too much loss of effect. Some of the other plants chosen for this blue and yellow group also involve taking a slight risk, but none of them is difficult to keep alive provided the weather does not turn extreme.

The safer, but duller, alternative to the mimosa might be a large lemon-yellow cephalaria, rather like a scabious, which would flower off and on all summer. The melianthus and the azara have stronger constitutions than the mimosa, but they too might need renewing after an exceptionally cold winter. Azara is an evergreen shrub which grows in the shape of a fishbone and has tiny puffs of pale yellow vanilla-scented flowers early in the year. Like the mimosa, it has leaves which will not shame this restrained summer colour scheme of pale blues and yellows, with a little backing from grey. Melianthus is also more remarkable for its leaves than for its

Cephalaria gigantea

(giant scabious)

In a warm place the winter flowers of mimosa would grace this border, which has plenty of cold weather interest as well as a

sustained scheme of yellow and blue throughout the rest of the year, though its colours are never strong.

flowers. In a hard winter plants may die back to ground level, but a little protection will keep them alive underground, ready to make six feet of blue-green growth the following year.

When the tulips and camassias are almost over the first wave of colour will wash across this planting, from the airy cream petals of *Rosa hugonis* to the lemon-cool peony. Both bear single flowers and the rose has filigree leaves, so the effect is light, more a watercolour than an oil. Behind them the ceanothus is covered with smoky clusters of pale blue in early summer and there is stronger colour from delphiniums and geraniums, backed up by washed-lavender polemonium.

With the irises and campanulas, these

keep the colours going until the roses take over. 'Tynwald' is a newish cream-coloured hybrid tea, with full flowers and glossy leaves. It needs hard pruning to keep it from growing too tall, but it is sturdy, long-flowering and disease-free. I cannot think why it is not more popular. After its first flush of blooms 'Alister Stella Gray' continues to throw up the odd flower throughout the summer.

Thalictrum and fennel are included to add height and lightness to the picture. Like all the plants in this small space they will need disciplining to keep them in scale. Both will cause problems if they are allowed to seed. The summer should finish with porcelain-blue salvias and cream-

Campanula persicifolia

■

Acacia dealbata

(mimosa)

coloured daisies, as well as clematis in blue and yellow forms. Evening primroses in the perennial but pale form can be fitted in to any gaps if the element of blue is felt to be too strong, and all flowers, including the gentian-blue delphiniums, will need dead-heading to keep them in the picture. With regular grooming and feeding Belladonna delphiniums, unlike their taller relations, ought to flower throughout the summer.

If you want flowers to work overtime to create this sort of effect you have to be prepared to give them plenty of attention. Left to its own devices a group of plants like this will certainly perform, but to put on a real show they require some dedication. The ceanothus, azara, mimosa and melianthus will need watching, because if they are allowed to dominate the effect of understated colour will be diminished. All the clematis will need severe pruning so as to allow the winter shrubs to be seen, and the roses will need to be well cared for if they are to be the mainstay of the summer.

Camassia cusickii

■

Polemonium caeruleum

(Jacob's ladder)

Tulipa 'West Point'

with *Brunnera macrophylla*

Rosa hugonis

(golden rose of China)

Gold and White, Shrubs for Shade

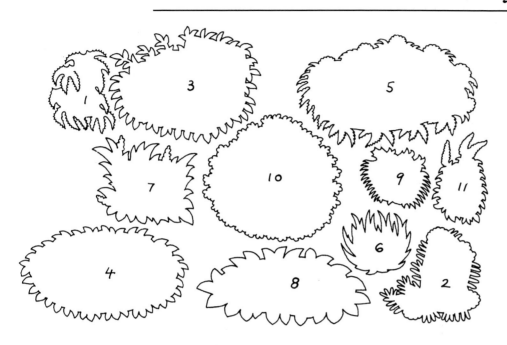

Early

1 *Helleborus lividus corsicus*
  (hellebore)
2 *Euphorbia amygdaloides robbiae*
  (wood spurge)
3 *Cornus alba* 'Elegantissima' (dogwood)

Early-mid

4 *Philadelphus coronarius* 'Aureus'
  (mock orange)
5 *Sambucus racemosa* 'Plumosa Aurea'
  (cut-leaf elder) underplanted with
  Cyclamen coum album (early)
6 *Iris* 'Florentina'

Mid

7 *Veratrum album*
8 *Hosta fortunei albopicta*
9 *Lilium martagon album*
  (turk's-cap lily)

Mid-late

10 *Rosa* 'Golden Wings' underplanted
   with *Narcissus* 'Thalia' (early)
11 *Lysimachia clethroides* (loosestrife)

A coat of yellow paint indoors can do wonders for a north-facing room, creating the illusion of sunshine where no sun ever shines. A splash of gold in the garden can have a similar effect. Luckily, as the sun tends to scorch their leaves, the fierce light of gold and variegated shrubs is better suited to shade, so they can be used to illuminate the darker recesses of the garden. This group might grow in a place where the sun never penetrates, in a town basement area or under some gloomy but not too dense trees. The famous English gardener Alvilde Lees Milne planted golden philadelphus under the canopy of a giant cedar tree (until the tree was blown down in a storm), making her garden look in spring as though the sun was shining under dark branches, and providing a brilliant example for others to copy. Sadly it is rare to see people taking advantage of the fact that plants for shade and ground cover need not be dull.

This planting is trouble-free and might take one, or at most two, days a year to maintain as it stands. The star attraction is the cut-leaf golden elder. This form grows more slowly than the common golden elder (*Sambucus aurea*) and its leaves are bronze when they first open. Those who want to see yellow at the start of the year, or cannot bear to wait for the showier version to grow, should settle for the common form, which will not disappoint anyone. It will however lack the finesse of its more distinguished relations. Small gardens deserve a policy of nothing but the best. Such attention to detail may sound demanding, but patience while waiting for things to mature and diligence in searching out the perfect plant for a scheme are among the most desirable virtues of the discriminating gardener.

The other large shrub in the picture is the cornus, which has sealing-wax-red stems to cheer you through the winter and white-splashed leaves all summer. It will need to have old stems cut back annually to keep it in scale and also to encourage the sealing wax output, for only the young branches are really red. The rose 'Golden Wings' is dependable in shade, where

Cornus alba

'Elegantissima' (dogwood)

it will not flower very much, but its sporadic single blooms are a pleasure whenever they appear, which happens over quite a long period.

If you have opted for the long wait and the bronze spring of *Sambucus racemosa*, the early leaves of a bush of golden philadelphus will compensate for any lack of gold. But as the elder's leaves turn yellow, so the philadelphus will start to fade. They are never so bright as they are early in the year, and by midsummer they will have become an ordinary green. If you wanted to make more of the area you could keep the philadelphus hard-pruned, by cutting out all old wood every year, so that a variegated periwinkle could be seen at its feet. This is not something to attempt if you like to leave the balance of power to nature, because the periwinkle will soon throttle the philadelphus if it is left to its own devices.

The herbaceous plants chosen here are easy and will look good for most of the year. The veratrum, with large green leaves pleated like a Fortuny dress, needs protection from slugs, as does the hosta. As they divert the eye from dwelling too long on the passenger philadelphus, the large leaves of these two plants play an important part in the picture, and it would be a pity to let this planned element be wrecked by a slug. The iris (the variety that provides the orris root for pot-pourri) seems happy to flower in shade and provides a small exclamation mark next to the euphorbia (which is the one that Miss Robb found growing in the Balkans and brought home in one of

Euphorbia amygdaloides robbiae

(wood spurge)

Sambucus racemosa

'Plumosa Aurea' (cut-leaf elder)

Veratrum album

(white false hellebore)

her hatboxes). The rounded *Euphorbia polychroma* might have been a better choice of shape, but its flowers are much more acid in colouring. I would therefore choose the dark green *E. robbiae*, with its lime-green flowers, which will ultimately not mind being shaded out by the golden elder. Lime green too are the flowers of the Corsican hellebore, which deserves a place in the record book for its five-month-long performance. Apart from the flowering of the rose and the vertical interest provided by white veratrum, loosestrife and martagon lilies, not much will happen to this arrangement in the summer months. But the elder puts up a powerful display and the planting will provide an interesting if unspectacular backdrop to illuminate a difficult corner.

Hosta fortunei albopicta

■

Lysimachia clethroides

(loosestrife)

Iris

'Florentina'

Golden and variegated foliage and flowers in white and yellow create the illusion of sunlight where there is little. In summer, the yellow-greens of the philadelphus and cut-leaf elder are lightened by the white-splashed leaves of dogwood and hosta. (Mid)

MIXED COLOURS

A RESTRICTED PALETTE MAY BE EASIER TO
manage than the full range of colours, and pastel
shades are another safe option, but mixing
flowers in all the colours of the rainbow
is irresistible.

*Most gardeners' inclination is to play safe
with pastels, but this inspired handling of
bright colours by the National Trust at
Snowshill Manor shows the brilliant effect
you can achieve with a strong mixture.*

Opposite: A hundreds-and-thousands, or kaleidoscopic, effect such as this is not as casually achieved as it might appear. This method of handling a number of bright colours relies on plenty of white to separate strong shades.

Monet designed much of his multicoloured garden at Giverny to be seen against the back-ground of pink and green provided by his house. This pairing of irises with strong yellow wallflowers is typical of the vivid colour combinations of which Monet was fond: among his favourites were nasturtiums with gladioli and lupins with sunflowers.

$\mathcal{K}$aleidoscopes of colour are hard to arrange in small gardens. Gertrude Jekyll had yards of borders through which she graded bands of one hue after another. This might be called the rainbow technique, for which modern gardeners do not have the scope or the space. A kaleidoscopic, or a hundreds-and-thousands approach, is not much more suitable, although cottage gardeners seem sometimes to manage to mix all the primary and many of the secondary colours together in one border, not in blocks or bands but in ones and twos with plenty of green and white. Experiments with this technique have sometimes proved brilliant (in both the literal and the colloquial sense), but a couple of years of lack of colour censorship in one part of the garden should be enough to convince any gardener that this is not the best way of presenting flowers. The principle of combining one of each plant that you like together in one place is not usually enough to give a group cohesion. Personal taste is notoriously fickle; the plant which caught your eye in someone else's garden last week may not be the best neighbour for the one which you admired at the flower show last summer. Nor will these two be improved by the addition of

Opposite left: The
scarlet window frame
and whitewashed
walls of this house,
echoed in the bright
primaries of roses,
lupins and peonies,
make a much more
bracing background
than the muted
shades of Giverny.

a flower picked unseen from a seed catalogue with another shrub described in glowing terms by a friend. The wisdom of this eclectic approach began to seem suspect when I discovered in my own garden an annual rudbeckia 'Marmalade' (recommended by a gardening friend) next to a lilac achillea (admired in Beth Chatto's garden) and backed by the favourite scarlet dahlia 'Bishop of Llandaff'. The odd deliberate mistake, as an antidote to too much good taste, can enliven a garden – but not perhaps too odd.

Victorian colourists, whose legacy persists in gardens today, liked to use complementary colours for strong contrasts. This means that you use each primary colour with a secondary made of the other two primaries: yellow with purple (blue and red), red with green (blue and yellow) and blue with orange (yellow and red). For me these intense contrasts are too strong for everyday life and too dominant in borders where other colours are included. With the exception of blue and orange, where the cold-warm contrast is so beautifully balanced that it is exciting, I dislike combinations of complementary colours under temperate skies. But this is a personal veto: others may and do enjoy complementaries together. And I wonder whether the word complementary has gone some way towards prejudicing our taste, because it sounds like complimentary, suggesting flattery? What complementary means as a colour description is that colours that are opposite one another on the spectrum will annihilate each other when mixed together. This technical point may not appear relevant to garden planners, but the fact that a mixture of the pigments of these colours produces black could explain my lack of enthusiasm for groups of complementaries. An impression of black in the garden is not what most of us want to see.

Harmonies based on one primary, with only an occasional accent of contrast, are safest in small spaces, where a restricted palette is easier to manage than a riot of colour. But for gardeners who want to attempt something more ambitious there are tricks which can help them to combine shades that are based on more than one primary. The best of these is to use two colours as major players and to restrict the others to supporting roles. Using four or five colours at full blast and in equal quantities is not a recipe for success. If the main colours are at full strength, the supporting

Opposite right: Blue
is present in all the
colours in this picture
in a delicate harmony
composition: the
leaves and buds of
the poppy contain
plenty of blue in their
green, and there is
also some blueing of
the crimson tissue-
paper petals, which
tones with the pale
crane's-bill behind.

Opposite below: In
this painter's garden
in London the sugary
pink of the cistus is
tempered by touches
of red from the
'Marjorie Fair' roses
and the vermilion
spires of lupins.

ones should be reduced not just in number but also in strength. But when the dominant colours are pale, the occasional bright flash of contrast can bring a planting to life.

If, for example, you imagine a border based on a primary colour (red, blue or yellow) with another strong colour made up of the same primary and one other (purple, green or orange), the third colour that you could safely add to these would be a pale version of the third primary, that is the one not included in the make-up of the colours already chosen. A group of plants where blue and green were emphasized, for example, might not be improved by the addition of red, but pink would offend no one. Similarly, if the dominant colours were red and purple, pale yellow would be a happier choice than gold, as it would with a

The clear red of the penstemon in the foreground here dominates the blued pinks and lavender-blues in the rest of the border. If the blue of the catmint contained less pink the result would be less restful and more startling.

blue and purple scheme. The same principle applied to combinations of red and orange or yellow and orange flowers would allow you to use pale blue more easily than a richer shade.

Another way of keeping colours to acceptable levels is to use plenty of white. Painters know about the 'spreading' effect, seen at its most extreme when colours are placed on a black or dark background. White has the opposite effect: surrounded by white, colours keep their separate identities and are unaffected by neighbouring hues. Bright red flowers next to bright blue ones will merge into a heavy purple, but separated by white they keep their freshness. This is harder to do in a flowerbed than it is in a painting, but if there is enough white its presence will stop colours from muddying one another.

Masses of white campanulas here keep the rest of the colours very quiet and separate. Using white will allow you to combine any colours you wish, even clashing ones.

The introduction of plenty of white makes this planting seem brighter than the one opposite, even though the colours of the flowers are actually dimmer than those in the border at Crathes.

Opposite: At Crathes Castle in Scotland misty borders of banked summer colour blend into a soothing composition of grey-blues.

In small borders, where broad splashes of white would take up too much room, you can probably add white to a planting vertically. There may not be enough space for a clump of long-flowering daisies, but there is nearly always room for a few foxgloves or some loosestrife. Even delphiniums (especially the smaller-flowered Belladonna forms) give you more flowers for the area they occupy than a perennial like a peony, which fills the bed laterally with its rounded dome shape. On a much smaller scale plants like *Omphalodes linifolia*, a slender annual, *Heuchera* 'Greenfinch' or the white asphodel can also add white to a group of flowers without filling too much space.

Where a constant white presence is needed to keep colours from colliding variegated leaves can be useful, and can often look fresher than greys. Delacroix objected to grey because it diminished colours. He was right; too much grey can make colours murky, because one of the properties of grey is that it assumes the complementary colour of its neighbour. So next to red flowers, grey leaves look greener; and near yellow ones they are tinged with purple, which brings about a deadening and darkening effect. For this reason the popular *Senecio* 'Sunshine' is often live-headed by sensitive gardeners, who find its

Misty lavender-blues, mauves and pinks are given yet another twist by touches of lemon yellow from thalictrum and santolina.

This original group of deep purple roses with creamy yellow roses and white peonies makes an interesting change from the more usual pastel shades of pink and blue.

combination of grey leaves with bright yellow daisies unappealing. This is not just because the daisies appear too bright in borders where other flowers are grown, for I have seen senecios shorn of daisies in isolated places too. I suspect it has more to do with an involuntary revulsion against the deadening effect of complementary purple-grey leaves against the yellow flowers. Proper silvers, rather than dull pewter-greys, are better as a foil for bright hues if you want to keep colours strong, because they show them at their truest and do not darken them. Where brightness is the aim, splashes of white variegation on shrubs such as *Cornus elegantissima* or *Pittosporum* 'Garnettii' or the silver leaves of mulleins and thistles are better allies in mixed borders than the dead greys of plants like senecio.

Perhaps the last ally of the colour addict is time. If you love rich colours but your garden is small, you can enjoy a rainbow of flowers in sequence. As the year passes one range of colours can give way to another without any discordance. As the simple shrub border included here shows, clear bright magenta and blue with silver and white in spring can give way to the misty pinks, greys and greens of summer, before turning finally to the glowing orange-reds of autumn.

Old-fashioned roses which have no orange in their make-up are easy to combine in an informal mixture, as here at the Lime Kiln Rosarium.

Opposite: Pink and blue with touches of white remain a trad-itional favourite for summer gardens. Rosa 'Surpasse Tout', long-flowering and bright pink, here adds life to a safe, old-fashioned scheme.

Pink, Purple and Grey Shrubs

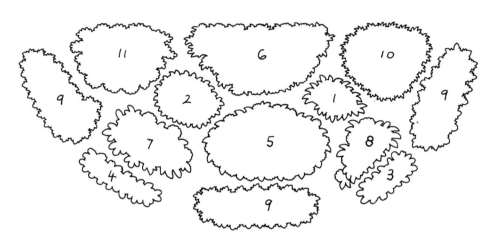

Suggested underplanting throughout:
Cyclamen coum and *Anemone blanda*
'White Splendour'

*A group of early shrubs and perennials
provides three separate colour schemes in a
year, and does not demand a place in the
sun. In early summer apple blossom colours
and rich pinks are mixed with greens.*
(Early-mid)

Early
1 *Rubus cockburnianus*
2 *Salix hastata* 'Wehrhahnii'
3 *Primula vulgaris* 'Alba Plena'
   (double white primrose)
4 *Primula* 'Wanda'
5 *Viburnum carlessii* 'Diana'

Early-mid
6 *Pyracantha* 'Watereri' (firethorn)
7 *Paeonia lactiflora* 'Instituteur Doriat'
   (peony)
8 *Paeonia lactiflora* 'Félix Crousse'
9 *Geranium macrorrhizum*
   'Ingwersen's Variety'

Mid-late
10 *Abelia* x *grandiflora*
11 *Rosa* 'Frau Dagmar Hastrup'

The colour scheme in a garden need not stay the same all through the year: this group illustrates a shift from magenta, pink, white and silver in early spring to pale pink, white and grey in summer, then ends the year with scarlet berries and rosy leaves for autumn and early winter.

The magenta flowers of the primrose 'Wanda' and spring-flowering *Cyclamen coum*, with the white-stemmed bramble and silver catkins of the willow, make a strong start to the year. Later these colours could look artificial, like decorations left over from Christmas, but before the leaves clothe the trees they look bright and sparkling, which is a help when days are sombre.

The pitch of these could be further tuned by adding more bulbs. Early in the year is the time for short bursts of colour which are too garish for summer. Patches of dark blue grape hyacinths, scillas and snowdrops could crowd under the skirts of later-flowering deciduous plants to make a bright start in spring. Another year, yellow dwarf daffodils and primroses could be added instead of blue bulbs, and colour addicts might try blue, yellow, purple and white all at once, returning to the more sophisticated mixture of magenta, white and silver after a year or two of carnival colours.

Whatever the bulbs chosen, the fat unfurling leaves of peonies, like small red hands, will provide an extra splash of colour. Slow to settle, peonies like rich and undisturbed living, but it is often forgotten that in addition to their blowsy flowers they give good value throughout the year, at first with their buds and unfolding leaves, then with strong foliage which turns red in autumn. However, botrytis can disfigure their leaves and rot them before they reach the autumn, and if this is a risk you will need to take action. Removing flower stalks before they have a chance to seed can keep the plant strong, but in extreme cases spraying is the only answer.

When spring is over the apple-blossom looks of pale pink and white viburnum and the ground-covering geranium make a gentler picture. The peonies bloom in luscious summer pinks, and as they fade they are replaced by a gentler colour scheme. The long-flowering abelia has flowers which are not showy, but they do provide a green and white background

Rosa

'Frau Dagmar Hastrup'

to the rose which keeps going all through the summer. The misty pink single flowers of the rugosa rose, with its crinkled green leaves, are soothing rather than stimulating. Rugosas are the easiest of all roses to grow because they rarely succumb to pests or diseases. The double forms, like 'Blanc Double de Coubert', stand out in the garden better than the single varieties. They are not as good at producing hips, however, and here this is a consideration. As autumn arrives, the colours

Lacquer-red berries and rosehips with the pinky leaves of peonies make quite a different composition in autumn. The berries should hang on for months if the birds will leave them alone. (Mid-late)

Cyclamen coum

brighten again. The peony leaves turn to brilliant reds, the rose bears tomato-coloured hips and the pyracantha is covered in lacquer-red berries; and so the atmosphere of sleepy summer days becomes charged with autumn fireworks. Even the geranium, so leafy and modest for the rest of the year, puts on a show of russet leaves.

This group of plants is among the easiest to maintain of all the collections in this book. The rose is of the type that needs minimal pruning: a little old wood can be cut out each year. The willow and the bramble also perform better on newer wood, and primroses do better divided each year. Otherwise, apart from a slight risk of the geraniums running all over the bed, most plants can be left to grow at their own pace with very little interference.

■

Anemone blanda

'White Splendour'

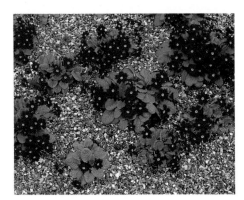

Primula

'Wanda'

Paeonia lactiflora

'Félix Crousse' (peony)

Geranium macrorrhizum

'Ingwersen's Variety'

Viburnum carlesii

'Diana'

Clear Blues and Pinks

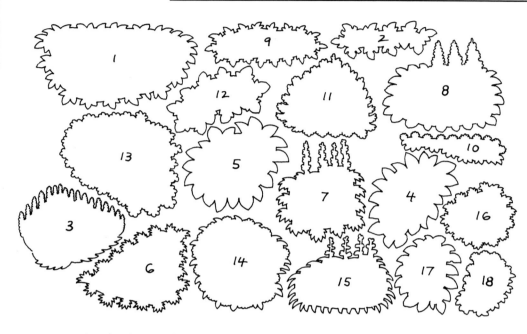

Suggested underplanting throughout: *Tulipa* 'Palestrina' and *T. clusiana* (lady tulip)

Early-mid

1 *Weigela* 'Florida Variegata'
2 *Humulus lupulus aureus* (golden hop)
3 *Salvia* x *superba* 'May Night'

Mid

4 *Digitalis lutea* (yellow foxglove)
5 *Digitalis* x *mertonensis*
6 *Geranium sanguineum* 'Glenluce'
7 *Delphinium* Belladonna 'Wendy'
8 *Salvia sclarea turkestanica* underplanted with *Myosotis alpestris* (forget-me-not) or *M.* 'Blue Ball' (early-mid)

Mid-late

9 *Clematis* 'Perle d'Azur'
10 *Felicia amelloides*
11 *Perovskia atriplicifolia*
12 *Alcea rugosa*, syn. *Althaea rugosa* (hollyhock)
13 *Rosa* 'Nathalie Nypels' underplanted with *Myosotis* 'White Ball' (forget-me-not)
14 *Helichrysum* 'Sulphur Light'
15 *Penstemon* 'Apple Blossom'
16 *Geranium* 'Ann Folkard'
17 *Nicotiana langsdorfii* (tobacco plant)
18 *Osteospermum barberae* 'Blue Streak', syn. *Dimorphotheca barberae* (cape marigold)

There have been times in my own garden in early summer when pink has been the dominant colour. The pink, white and green combination found in apple blossom is, I suspect, universally pleasing, and many of us subconsciously fall back on this group of colours as a base in the garden. Pink is a warm and unthreatening colour which it is natural to like. But because it is safe we tend to choose it first, missing out on more original combinations like the one illustrated here, which is inspired by an existing border in a modern Dutch garden.

Clear blues, with a little magenta, a few silver pinks and lemon yellows and splashes of white, make a lovely summer group which is more original than many traditional borders. Apple-blossom pink and green do make an appearance here, in the penstemon and the long-flowering geranium 'Glenluce', but they do not in any way dominate the scheme.

There is pink, too, in the lovely *Salvia turkestanica*, which adds spires of silver-pink to the picture. This plant has an odd smell if you crush or bruise it: although some people love it, others may find it rather too pungent, so it is not perhaps the plant to site next to a path where you might be constantly brushing against it. It is also a biennial, but usually seeds itself. More pink, white and green comes from the variegated weigela, whose cream-edged leaves make a good background for other flowers after its own pale pink ones have faded in early summer.

The sweetness of the pinks is spiced up by a flash of strong magenta from the other hardy geranium 'Anne Folkard', as well as by the strength of the clear blues which are the base colour of the border. *Clematis* 'Perle

A mixed planting in a Dutch garden where clear blues and pinks dominate, with some support from grey and sulphur yellow. Airy spires of vertical colour from foxgloves and delphiniums keep the planting light in feeling.

d'Azur' grown through the golden hop looks brighter than it does when grown with pink flowers, which tend to turn its blue to violet. The late-flowering perovskia gives the impression of a group of silvery-lavender spires. Its white stems make the flowers appear more blue than they really are. There is, however, no confusion about the Belladonna delphiniums, which are the colour of gentians. These airy columns

of flowers are not at all like show delphiniums: it is hard to obtain named varieties, but they come easily from seed. The trick is to grow your own and select the best and brightest form for yourself. Judicious dead-heading can keep them flowering for two months on end, and if cut down and fed and watered as the last spires fade they will often appear again in autumn. It may however be better to rely on the

penstemon and the perovskia to cover up for what can be a rather weak performance late in the year, allowing them to grow towards one another across the gap left by the delphinium.

A large quota of tall plants is included here, because where space is short these vertical flowers can provide colour which would not fit laterally. Two different foxgloves and the single hollyhock provide columns of strawberry pink and pale yellows. Unlike most of their relations, these foxgloves are reliably perennial. *D. × mertonensis* is best divided after flowering to keep it in good heart. Lower down the scale, the salvia's bracts add further to the impression that the border is crowded with colour. Summer effects are the aim of this planting. It includes nothing for winter, so it is not one to choose if it is to be the only border in the garden – unless of course you never look outside in the cold months of the year.

Digitalis lutea

(yellow foxglove)

Penstemon

'Apple Blossom'

Perovskia atriplicifolia

'Blue Spire'

A mixed summer border based on blues is more original than one where pink dominates. This one was inspired by an existing planting in a modern Dutch garden. (Mid-late)

Misty Pinks and Blues

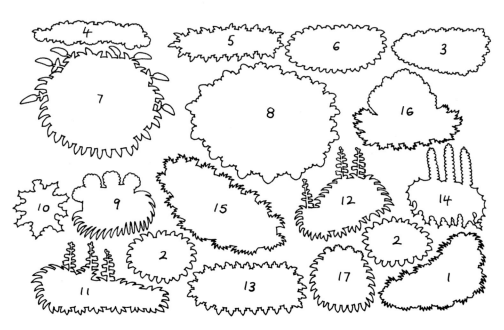

Mid

1 *Dianthus* 'Prudence'
2 *Lychnis coronaria alba* (campion)
3 *Rosa* 'Mme Isaac Pereire'

Mid-late

4 *Solanum crispum* 'Glasnevin'
   (Chilean potato tree)
5 *Clematis* 'Huldine'
6 *Escallonia* 'Iveyi'
7 *Buddleja davidii* 'Black Knight'
8 *Lavatera olbia* 'Burgundy Wine'
   (tree mallow)
9 *Agapanthus* 'Headbourne Hybrids'
10 *Silybum marianum* (milk thistle)
11 *Penstemon* 'Sour Grapes' underplanted
    with *Tulipa* 'Estella Rijnveld' (early)
12 *Penstemon* 'Garnet' underplanted with
    Tulipa 'Angélique' (early)
13 *Verbena* 'Sissinghurst' underplanted
    with *Tulipa clusiana* (lady tulip/early)
14 *Acanthus spinosus*
    (bear's breeches)
15 *Artemisia* 'Powis Castle'

Late

16 *Perovskia atriplicifolia*
17 *Aster* x *thompsonii* 'Nanus'

This group reverses the emphasis in the preceding arrangement, as the base colour here is rich pink. Where blue dominated before, now pinks shading to crimson and burgundy are the colour images that remain.

The rose-tinted look is easy to achieve when its centrepiece is a shrub that is in flower from midsummer to autumn. This is one of the new non-stop lavateras (in a darker shade than the traditional form) that have become an indispensable feature of summer borders. Darker still is the buddleia 'Black Knight', which has flowers of a strong violet. As this collection also includes the richest of pink roses, deep purple-red penstemons, intense blue agapanthus and the shocking pink verbena 'Sissinghurst' there is plenty of strong colour. A patch of grey made by the loveliest of the artemisias, 'Powis Castle', keeps this combination from looking flashy. White flowers in place of the all grey leaves here would give an effect that was fresher and brighter but less well balanced. But the greys of artemisia, lychnis, silybum and perovskia all help to tone down these vivid plants, bringing their colours into a quieter harmony. If there were fewer grey plants they might jump out of the picture, but in this number they blur in the background.

Some white has been included, however, in the escallonia next to the florid pink rose 'Mme Isaac Pereire', and in the flowers of the grey-leaved lychnis. 'Mme Isaac' is too strong for some tastes, but the perovskia goes some way towards softening it. The escallonia's white blossom will only occasionally appear at the same time as the roses, as 'Mme Isaac' takes a rest after the first midsummer bloom until the autumn.

The lychnis, which here is white-flowered, could have been chosen in its magenta version if more pink were wanted, but this might be rather wasted against the penstemon. This is the sort of detail which it is fun to adjust over the years, because in the end all

Agapanthus

'Headbourne Hybrids'

The fat pink of the old-fashioned mallow among a heady summer mixture of dark purple buddleia and blue agapanthus. Blue daisies and silver leaves crowd the front of the border.

companion planting is a matter of personal taste. The white clematis 'Huldine', too, would be my own preference over other possible choices, such as the pink 'Lady Balfour' or 'Comtesse de Bouchaud', which is more mauve. Both would keep the scheme to pinks and blues, but might in my view make it all rather cloying. A compromise might be to use a grey plant at the back. *Rosa glauca* has insignificant pink button-sized flowers, but in sun its leaves are blue-grey, and

late in the year it bears hips. This would work better with more space than is shown here, however. In a tight situation the tree germander (*Teucrium fruticans*), with silver-grey leaves and small pale blue flowers throughout the summer, could be trained up the wall.

In mixed colour groups quite small adjustments can change the emphasis of a planting. This one could be made mistier with more grey plants, or brighter with the addition of more white and lemon yellow. Or with very

little alteration the blues could be increased so that the pinks looked more mauve than rosy: if, for example, a clump of the long-flowering *Aster × frikartii* were substituted for the penstemons, lychnis and small aster 'Nanus', even the 'Burgundy Wine' mallow would start to look more blue than maroon. The possibilities and permutations are endless, as they are in all these designs.

■

SEASONAL
COLOURS

COLOURS CHANGE WITH LIGHT AND
seasons: winter brings cut-glass definition to
stems and leaves; the watercolour skies of spring
freshen everything in the garden; hot summer
days call for a rich mix of colours and the slanting
light of autumn casts a misty haze everywhere.

Slanting autumn sunlight mellows all
bright colours, so that even scarlet rose hips
have a gentler appearance than they would
when the sun is at its zenith.

*D*ifferent seasons suit different colours. As the light changes throughout the year, so does our reaction to what we see. Winter is a time for silvers and greys, for opalescent snowdrops and blue cabbage leaves. It is also the moment when green comes into its own. In winter, evergreens, which are bleached into yellowishness by the strong suns of summer, look bluer and stronger under the weak rays of a declining solstice. The low light also enhances gold variegated leaves, or bright jasmine, which become themselves a source of light. This ability to illuminate relegates colour to a secondary feature. What you notice about yellow in winter is not so much that it is yellow but that it is bright, and this response is further strengthened by the power of association. Looking at a patch of yellow in winter has the added attraction of suggesting the sunlight and warmth that fill summer gardens.

These sun substitutes often look better isolated, as they are early in the year, than they do when surrounded by other plants. This is as it should be, because this is the time of year to appreciate the beauty of a single plant or flower. Any flower that blooms in winter is a rarity, and will merit closer inspection than it would later in the year, when abundance rules. The best winter light is

SEASONAL COLOURS 123

clear, bringing cut-glass definition to stems and leaves. Thus the outlines of plants are etched in air, rather like engravings, as they never are in summer, when everything blurs into an impressionistic haze. This has the effect of focusing the eye on simple features, so that a single white hellebore, protected from mud and slugs, can be enough to satisfy an onlooker who might be more demanding at any other time of year.

Like yellow, white is valuable in winter not just as a change of hue, but also for the light it brings to the darkened garden. A thicket of the ghostly bramble *Rubus cockburnianus* would not rate a second glance in summer, but in the bare months of the year the silver stems stand out like wands of tungsten. Other colours which fade into the background for the rest of the year assume a new distinction in winter. The lacquer-red stems of *Cornus alba* 'Westonbirt', the squirrel-red trunk of yew, and every shade of brown and grey on the trunks and branches of trees and shrubs, please winter eyes attuned to sparse effects.

Spring light makes everything look fresh, so that even a pink and blue colour scheme looks original. The addition of a splash of red also helps to make this group of tulips and forget-me-nots a little more special.

If winter light lends colours distinction, spring brings them purity. Yellows and blues never seem so innocent as they do in spring, when they take on the translucence of a watercolour painting. In winter a common primrose plant would appear predominantly green (a good green containing plenty of blue) with flowers tending more to white than yellow. In summer and autumn the same plant might look undistinguished, with the greeny-yellow tones of flower and leaf merging; but in spring the primrose comes alive. For this is the only time of the year when the pale hues of leaf and flower really balance one another, to be seen at their freshest. It is also the moment when the soft greens of emerging leaves give a pale aura to every planting, rather like reflections in water. This is an effect which can be used to advantage. Such clarity is hard to come by later in the year, when all the leaves have turned to the green of cooked spinach and the air is muddied with heat. Half shades are clearer in spring: the blue-pink flowers of pulmonaria are just that, not purple, but

The pink and white blossom of cherry and magnolia, with tender green grass and the yellow of emerging leaves, is enough to suggest spring.

The washed yellow of primroses with the intense blue of grape hyacinths make another well-tried spring formula. It is interesting to compare the effect of this with the ceanothus and yellow rose on page 88.

partly blue and partly pink, while the washed-out 'dirty' pink of ribes, the common flowering currant, is saved from dinginess by the gentle light of spring. Even oranges, which later will look burnished and metallic, have no trace of hardness in spring.

As the season progresses and the sun strengthens, colours lose their spring freshness and become richer. The mingling and merging of flowery colours, until it is hard to tell them apart, is a feature of summer gardens. There are rich fat pinks in variety, and mauves, lilacs and purples, as well as crimsons, salmons and scarlets. With so many gradations of colour it needs a positive effort to group them so that they do one another justice. There is, too, the effect of the sun on green which Ruskin observed: 'For instance: when grass is lighted strongly by the sun in certain directions it is turned from green into a peculiar and somewhat dusty looking yellow.' Summer greens tend to the greenery-yallery, and if they are not to tinge and subdue other colours it is important to compensate for this. Strong flower colour is one way of tackling the problem. The two schemes which rely on annuals for their main impact do so for good reasons, because continuous colour from flowers can help to limit the influence of green. But more subtle effects, using intermittent flowers in less positive

'Rich colours of early summer, with scarlet poppies against white crambe, make a grand and immaculately kept border at Jenkyn Place. It is also fairly straightforward to maintain, as it is based on easy plants.

Lavender-blues, rather than the clear blues of early spring, suggest the heat of summer days. Here agapanthus and catmint are complemented by greens with a high blue content. The problem with so many greens in summer is that the sun brings out the yellow in them.

colours, need variations in leaf colour and size to outweigh the green factor. Modern gardeners often resort to silver foliage to alleviate the monotony of green, but this can produce its own problems. If an excess of green deadens a border, too much silver can damage its unity. Employed as subtly as the touches of white that a painter uses to highlight a picture, silver can be lovely, but a heavy hand will not improve a border any more than it would a painting. Harsh contrasts can be reduced by including some transitional greys (more blue than silver). A patch of artemisia near pink old-fashioned roses, for example, has become a garden cliché, but this association can sometimes be too strong for the feeling of a border. Lavender, catmint and 'Jackman's Blue' rue will often make less abrupt transitions for the eye than would

The white garden at Tintinhull has plenty of dark green backing against which irises and pure white stocks stand out like silhouettes. The perennial stock has a long flowering season and good, subtle grey leaves.

silver plants when a gentler summer arrangement is wanted.

Slanting sunlight makes warm colours acceptable once more in the autumn garden. Once the sun has passed its zenith yellow can be used again without fear of brassiness, and tawny reds and oranges are also improved by the mellow light of shorter days. The last burst of flowers before winter sets in has an added poignancy: this is the time of year when you want to be prodigal with colour. Bright blue ceratostigma, shocking pink nerines and the cerise salvia 'Bethellii' can all be combined with no fear of brashness; they suit Indian summers which slide into winter with no autumnal mid-season. But when there is that hint of brown in the air that signals the decline of the year, then the russet tones of late daisies and chrysanthemums come into their own.

Throughout the year it is easy to recognize the seasonal changes in light which produce the dominant colour mood: sharp in winter, pure in spring, rich in summer and subtle in autumn. Understanding this and working with the prevailing light help the gardener to make the best choice of plants, not only for a particular situation but also for a specific time of year.

'The sear, the yellow leaf' of autumn, can make beautiful compositions, as this arrangement in a range of greyed browns and russets shows. It is a sad time of year and this picture says it all.

Opposite: Autumn can also be suggested by borders. Bronze and yellow daisies belong as much to the dying year as the most vividly turning trees.

The rosier image of autumn suggests fireworks, apples and bonfires. These two pictures show how powerfully colour can evoke different moods.

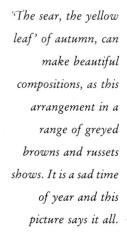

Blue and Yellow, Spring and Summer

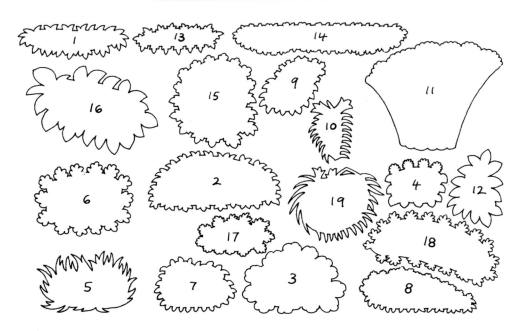

Suggested underplanting throughout: *Crocus etruscus* 'Zwanenburg', *Anemone blanda* 'Atrocaerulea', *Narcissus* 'February Gold' and *N.* 'Silver Chimes'

Early
1 *Prunus mume* 'Omoi-no-mama'
2 *Ribes laurifolium* (winter-flowering currant)
3 *Bergenia* 'Silberlicht'
4 *Doronicum plantagineum* 'Excelsum' (leopard's bane)

Early-mid
5 *Iris* 'Jane Phillips'
6 *Aquilegia vulgaris alba*
7 *Valeriana phu* 'Aurea' or *Tanacetum parthenium* (golden feverfew)
8 *Omphalodes cappadocica* (navelwort)

Mid
9 *Campanula lactiflora alba*
10 *Lilium regale* (regal lily)
11 *Spartium junceum* (Spanish broom)
12 *Digitalis purpurea alba* (white foxglove) or *Lysimachia ephemerum* (loosestrife)

Mid-late
13 *Clematis orientalis* 'Bill Mackenzie'
14 *Ceanothus* 'Burkwoodii' or C. 'Autumnal Blue'
15 *Anemone x hybrida* 'Honorine Jobert'
16 *Nicotiana sylvestris* (flowering tobacco)
17 *Malva* 'Primley Blue' or *Geranium* 'Buxton's Blue'
18 *Ruta graveolens* 'Jackman's Blue' (rue)
19 *Hemerocallis* 'Marion Vaughn'

*I*n spring yellow dominates this patch, with blue as the secondary colour. In summer their roles are reversed, the yellow being restricted to one area and surrounded by the soothing influence of misty blues and whites.

The start of the year sees grey-blue 'Zwanenburg' crocuses and blue anemones, followed by narcissi and the bright yellow daisies of doronicum. Less often seen is the winter-flowering currant, which has greenish-cream flowers. It is an obliging shrub which can become gawky with age, so it needs some pruning to give it a positive shape. A pool of yellow at the front of the border is provided by another uncommon plant: the point of this valerian is its bright yellow leaves in spring. Later in the year they fade to green, before dullish white flowers appear. Golden feverfew could have been chosen if the idea of more colour in summer appealed, but I think the valerian is better because the yellow needs to be played down. Feverfew can often be relied on to stay gold throughout the winter and it produces attractive daisy flowers in autumn, but it is not long-lived.

The brightest of the spring flowers is the blue omphalodes, which prefers shade and moist soil, but if it is planted almost under the rue its flowering should coincide with the rue's annual cutback. Then by the time the omphalodes is past its best and longing for shelter, the leaves of the rue will have grown enough to provide the cover it needs. Two-tier planting like this is an essential technique for limited space, and it does also mean that plants which do not normally like the same conditions can be encouraged to co-exist, as they might here.

Blossom from the Japanese apricot and bergenia flowers both come in the same shade of pinky white. Like the other white flowers which appear at intervals here throughout the year, they have the effect of drawing some of the attention away from blues and yellows. Using plenty of white can help to give other colours clearer identities. In one successful large herbaceous border that I know the owner never pays any attention to whether colours 'go' together, but instead relies on masses of white to keep the peace.

Summer is dominated by the long-flowering Spanish broom, which bears yellow scented pea flowers on wands of green. Putting it next to the bright blue ceanothus 'Burkwoodii' is daring and the effect might pall. *C.* 'Autumnal Blue' has flowers in a softer shade which could work better, but if a constant supply of campanulas, lilies and foxgloves (or lysimachia) can be kept up the contrast will look less raw. On the whole, one primary colour at full strength is generally enough and it is safer to opt for pale yellow with bright blue, or bright yellow with pale

In summer the same colours seem stronger, and the fountain of gold from Spanish broom lasts a good three months. (Mid-late)

PLAN: BLUE *and* YELLOW, SPRING *and* SUMMER 131

Prunus mume

'Omoi-no-mama'

Spartium junceum

(Spanish broom)

blue, than it is to pit them one against the other. Much also depends on where the plants are sited. With a whitewashed wall behind them, as well as some continuity of white flowers, the two primaries might make the backbone of an attractive group. A green hedge or a red-brick wall might make it all too much, but a silvery wooden fence could restore the balance.

Later in the summer there are other opportunities for two-tier planting. The first is offered by the climbing mallow 'Primley Blue', which shares a spot with the winter-flowering currant. Like all the best things it is not hardy, but its summer-long flowers make it worth searching out and keeping. Cuttings can be taken, and in the absence of a greenhouse they can overwinter on a windowsill. Alternatively, extravagance can prevail and a new plant can be bought (only one) each year. When compared with the money that some spend on bedding plants twice yearly this would not seem outrageous. A second chance to demonstrate resourceful two-tier work presents itself with the iris 'Jane Phillips'. This is the best of the blues, but unlike *I. pallida pallida* its leaves cannot be said to be an adornment to the summer garden. If the iris fans are cut back there should be room to grow one of the airy flaxes between the rhizomes. *Linum narbonense* is an attractive pale blue, but *L. perenne* is prettier and brighter. The choice here would depend on how the relationship between the ceanothus and Spanish broom was going. If the colours were heading towards crude confrontation the paler *L. narbonense* would probably be best. Neither is long-lived.

Omphalodes cappadocica

(navelwort)

Clematis orientalis

'Bill Mackenzie'

Malva

'Primley Blue'

Yellow and Orange, Spring and Autumn

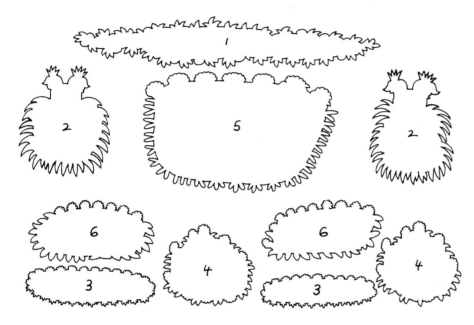

Underplanting throughout: *Tulipa acuminata*, *Narcissus* 'Tête-à-Tête' and *Chrysanthemum carinatum* 'Monarch Court Jesters' (syn. *C. tricolor*), *Salpiglossis sinuata* 'Splash', or *Dahlia* 'Coltness Hybrids'

Early

1 *Malus domestica* 'Discovery' (apple tree)
2 *Fritillaria imperialis* 'Lutea Maxima' (crown imperial)
3 *Iberis sempervirens* (candytuft)
4 *Cheiranthus cheiri* 'Wenlock Beauty' (wallflower)

Early-mid

5 *Euphorbia griffithii* 'Fireglow'
6 *Calendula officinalis* (pot marigold)

*L*ate summer and autumn are the times for tawny and sunset colours, but small gardens are not usually the ideal places to stage displays of autumn colour. A border like this provides a chance to enjoy some of the tints of turning leaves and ripening berries for those who do not run to a shrubbery or an arboretum.

This narrow arrangement might act as a division across a long thin town garden. Espaliered apples make good substitutes for hedges: as well as taking up less room than a conventional hedge they are ornamental and edible. The variety 'Discovery' has delicious early fruit, but there are also other good reasons for choosing it, as it earns its keep three times in a season.

Sunrise colours make a cheerful start to the year against a red-brick wall with an apple tree trained against it. (Early)

Apple blossom in spring is especially welcome in a small garden where there are inevitably limited possibilities for planting trees. In summer the fruit look pretty even before they are ripe, and when the apples have all been eaten 'Discovery' changes its appearance for the third time, as its leaves turn to a uniform rich yellow. There is one snag about planting an apple, however: it needs to be near another variety which flowers at the same time in order for cross-pollination to take place, otherwise it will not bear fruit. If neighbouring gardens are short on orchards, planting the small golden crab apple, *Malus* 'Golden Hornet', would be a possibility. A second espaliered apple chosen from those which flower in mid-season would be another solution to the problem.

In spring yellow crown imperials accompany the curious pointed petals of the horned *Tulipa acuminata* in a mixture of yellow, orange and green. Other flowers out at the same time here are the perennial wallflower 'Wenlock Beauty', a combination of orange and brown, and the euphorbia, which is predominantly green with terracotta flowers. Apple blossom and patches of white candytuft combine with the clear light of spring to keep all these oranges and yellows looking fresh and not at all end-of-summerish, as they might otherwise do.

Energetic gardeners will grow Iceland poppies to follow the crown imperials. They are not survivors, but generally seed themselves so that their orange, yellow and white flowers keep up a long display of colour on either side of the euphorbia until the summer annuals are ready to take over. This planting should have a splash of colour all through the year, otherwise there will be too much green.

The best candidates for this non-stop performance are of course the annuals which so many snobbish gardeners despise. They can be grown from seed and will flower from midsummer until the frosts. In small gardens it is better to concentrate on one variety for maximum effect: two clumps of whichever annuals you choose should each fill a space about a metre square.

The pot marigold tends to be passed over for showier forms, but is the easiest and most reliable of summer bedding plants provided it is frequently dead-headed. The petals can also be used in salads, which is another point in its favour.

Dahlias are traditional standbys for late summer colour and the 'Coltness Hybrids' are not too large, but pink shades should be avoided here for the sake of harmony. The annual chrysanthemum 'Monarch Court Jesters' includes brown in the autumnal shades of its flowers and would probably be my choice, but the beauty of annuals is that you can experiment with different varieties every year.

Nasturtiums (especially 'Empress of India'), variety rudbeckias (in spite of their name, 'Rustic Dwarfs' are worth growing) and nemesias all echo the bronzes, yellows and oranges of autumn leaves.

■

Calendula officinalis

(pot marigold)

Fritillaria imperialis

'Lutea Maxima' (crown imperial)

Euphorbia griffithii

'Fireglow'

Sunset colours for autumn under ripening apples finish the year with a warm glow. This is the time for tawny browns and oranges, as the slanting light of the dying year flatters all it touches. (Late)

Papaver nudicaule

(Iceland poppy)

Iberis sempervirens

(candytuft)

Malus domestica

'Discovery' (apple tree)

Narcissus

'Tête-à-Tête'

PLANT DIRECTORY

The plants on the following list of cultural hints are those which appear on plans throughout the book (numbers following the plant names are page references).

Abelia × grandiflora *112*
Semi-evergreen shrub
Midsummer-mid autumn
□ Thin older branches after flowering. Sheltered position and well-drained soil
3m/10ft

Abutilon × suntense *57*
Deciduous shrub
Late spring-early summer
□ Tender; sun or partial shade
5m/16ft

Abutilon vitifolium
'Veronica Tennant' *60*
Deciduous shrub
Summer
□ Sheltered site
4m/13ft

Acacia dealbata
(mimosa) *94, 96*
Evergreen, spreading tree
Winter-spring
□ Tender; full sun
12m/40ft

Acanthus balcanicus, syn.
A. longifolius
(bear's breeches) *35*
Perennial
Summer
□ Easy
60cm-1m/2-3ft

Acanthus spinosus *72, 73, 118*
Perennial
Summer
□ Any soil
1.2m/4ft

Achillea
'Moonshine' (yarrow) *92*
Upright perennial
Summer
□ Divide in spring
60cm/2ft

Aconitum vulparia
(monkshood) *92*
Perennial
Summer
□ Divide in autumn; moist soil
1-1.2m/3-4ft

Actinidia kolomikta *60*
Deciduous climber
Summer
□ Prune in winter
4m/13ft

Agapanthus
'Headbourne Hybrids' *118, 119*
Perennial
Late summer
□ Sun and moist soil
60-75cm/2ft-2ft 6in

Alcea rosea, syn.
Althaea rosea
single white (hollyhock) *77*
Biennial
Summer-early autumn
established
1.5m/5ft

Angelica archangelica *72*
Upright perennial
Summer
□ Sun or shade: remove seed-heads or treat as biennial
2m/6ft 6in

Antirrhinum
'Crimson Monarch'
(snapdragon) *54*
Annual
Summer
□ Rust-resistant
45cm/1ft 6in

Aquilegia alpina
(columbine) *32*
Perennial
Early summer
□ Sun or semi-shade
30cm/1ft

Aquilegia vulgaris *32*
Perennial
Early summer
□ Self-seeder
1m/3ft 3in

Aquilegia vulgaris alba
(white columbine) *130*
Perennial
Early summer
□ Seeds freely
1m/3ft 3in

Argyranthemum maderense *94*
Half-hardy perennial
Summer
□ Well-drained soil
23cm/9in

Artemisia arborescens *35*
Shrub
Summer-early autumn
□ Half-hardy; well-drained site; trim in spring
1m/3ft 3in

Artemisia
'Powis Castle' (wormwood) *77, 118*
Evergreen sub-shrub
Summer
□ Prune lightly in spring
1m/3ft 3in

Aster lateriflorus
'Horizontalis' *52*
Perennial
Autumn
□ Divide frequently
60cm/2ft

Aster × thompsonii
'Nanus' *32, 38, 118*
Perennial
Summer-autumn
□ Sun or shade; dead-head flowers
45cm/1ft 6in

Astrantia major
(masterwort) *72*
Perennial
Summer-autumn
□ Sun or semi-shade
60cm/2ft

Azara microphylla
(vanilla) *94*
Evergreen shrub, small tree

Alcea rosea
'Nigra' *54*
Perennial
Summer
□ Full sun; grow as biennial if rust is a problem
1.5-2m/5ft-6ft 6in

Alcea rugosa *115*
Short-lived perennial
Summer
□ Poor soil
1.5m/5ft

Alchemilla mollis
(lady's mantle) *74, 92*
Ground-cover perennial
Midsummer
□ Shade; cut back after flowering
50cm/1ft 8in

Anaphalis triplinervis
(pearl everlasting) *77, 78*
Dwarf perennial
Late summer
□ Sun or semi-shade; not too dry
20-30cm/8in-1ft

Anchusa capensis
'Blue Angel' *38*
Bushy biennial
Summer
□ Frost-tender
20cm/8in

Anemone blanda *32*
Tuber
Early spring
□ Semi-shade, well-drained soil
5-10cm/2-4in

Anemone blanda
'Atrocaerulea' *130*
Tuber
Spring
□ Semi-shade
5-10cm/2-4in

Anemone blanda
'White Splendour' *112, 114*
Tuber
Early spring
□ Sun or semi-shade; well-drained soil
5-10cm/2-4in

Anemone hupehensis japonica
'Prinz Heinrich' (Japanese anemone) *60*
Perennial
Late summer-early autumn
□ Invasive once established
1.2m/4ft

Anemone × hybrida
'Honorine Jobert' *32, 130*
Perennial
Late summer-early autumn
□ Semi-shade; easy when

□ Full sun; well-drained soil
1.5-2m/5ft-6ft 6in

Winter-spring
□ Tender; sun or shade
6m/20ft

Bergenia crassifolia *60*
Evergreen perennial
Spring
□ Sun or shade; divide in spring
30cm/1ft

Bergenia
'Silberlicht' *130*
Perennial
Spring
□ Shade
30cm/1ft

Buddleja davidii
'Black Knight' *118*
Deciduous shrub
Midsummer-autumn
□ Prune
5m/16ft 6in

Buddleja
'Lochinch' *35*
Deciduous shrub
Late summer-autumn
□ Full sun; slightly tender; cut back hard in spring
3m/10ft

Bupleurum fruticosum
(shrubby hare's ear) *72*
Evergreen bushy shrub
Midsummer-early autumn
□ Tender; sun or shade
2m/6ft 6in

Buxus suffruticosa
(dwarf box) *57*
Evergreen dwarf shrub
All year
□ Clip in early autumn
75cm/2ft 6in

Calendula officinalis
(pot marigold) *133, 134*
Annual
Spring-autumn
□ Dead-head to prolong flowering
60cm/2ft

Camassia cusickii *94, 96*
Bulb
Spring
□ Will naturalize
75cm-1m/2ft 6in-3ft 3in

Campanula lactiflora alba *77, 78, 130*
Perennial
Summer
□ Sun or shade
1.2m/4ft

Campanula persicifolia *94, 95*
Perennial
Summer
□ Sun or shade; divide regularly
1m/3ft 3in

Ceanothus
'Autumnal Blue' *130*
Shrub
Late spring-autumn
□ Frost-hardy; sheltered site, full sun, well-drained soil; cut out dead wood in spring; trim side shoots after flowering
3m/10ft

Ceanothus
'Burkwoodii' *130*
Evergreen shrub
Midsummer-mid autumn
□ Sheltered site; full sun; prune after flowering
1.5m/5ft

Ceanothus
'Cascade' *94*
Evergreen shrub
Late spring-early summer
□ Cut back after flowering; sheltered site
4m/13ft

Ceanothus impressus *32*
Evergreen shrub
Mid spring-early summer
□ Half-hardy; sheltered site; trim side shoots after flowering up to 2m/6ft 6in

Centranthus ruber
(valerian) *52*
Perennial
Late spring-autumn
□ Easy
60cm-1m/2ft-3ft 3in

Centranthus ruber albus
(white valerian) *77, 79*
Perennial
Recurrent
□ Poor conditions; self-seeder
60cm-1m/2ft-3ft 3in

Cephalaria gigantea
(giant scabious) *94, 95*
Perennial
Early summer
□ Sun and well-drained soil
2m/6ft 6in

Ceratostigma plumbaginoides *38*
Bushy perennial
Late summer-autumn
□ Sun and well-drained soil; cut out dead wood in spring
45cm/1ft 6in

Ceratostigma willmottianum *32*
Deciduous shrub
Late summer-autumn
□ Frost-tender; prune in spring
1m/3ft 3in

Cheiranthus cheiri
'Moonlight' (wallflower) *92*
Evergreen mat-forming perennial
Recurrent
□ Sunny site; poor soil
5cm/2in

Cheiranthus cheiri
'Vulcan' *52*
Semi-perennial
Spring
□ Renew frequently
up to 60cm/2ft

Cheiranthus cheiri
'Wenlock Beauty' *133*
Perennial
Spring
□ Renew from cuttings
up to 60cm/2ft

Chionodoxa luciliae
(glory of the snow) *35, 37*
Bulb

Early spring
□ Best in full sun
10-25cm/4-10in
Choisya ternata
(Mexican orange blossom) *72*
Evergreen shrub
Late spring, sometimes autumn
□ Frost-hardy
2.5m/8ft
Chrysanthemum carinatum
'Monarch Court Jesters', syn.
C. tricolor *133*
Branching annual
Summer
□ Sun; good soil
60cm/2ft
Clematis alpina
'Frances Rivis' *32*
Evergreen climber
Spring-early summer
□ Prune after flowering;
shady site
2-3m/6ft 6in-10ft
Clematis cirrhosa balearica *72*
Evergreen climber
Winter-spring
□ Shade roots
2-3m/6ft 6in
Clematis
'Huldine' *118*
Climber
Summer
□ Prune in early spring
3-4m/10-13ft
Clematis × jackmanii *32, 57*
Climber
Midsummer
□ Prune in early spring
3m/10ft
Clematis
'Jackmanii Superba' *36*
Climber
Midsummer
□ Prune in early spring
3m/10ft
Clematis × jouiniana
'Praecox' *72*
Sprawling sub-shrub
Late summer
□ Prune in early spring
1m/3ft 3in
Clematis
'Kermesina', syn. C. 'Viticella
Rubra' *60, 61*
Climber
Late summer
□ Prune in early spring
2-3m/6ft 6in-10ft
Clematis montana
'Elizabeth' *60*
Vigorous climber
Late spring
□ Cool wall; prune after
flowering
10-12m/33-40ft
Clematis
'Mrs Cholmondeley' *94*
Climber
Summer
□ Prune in early spring
2-3m/6ft 6in-10ft
Clematis orientalis
'Bill Mackenzie' *130, 132*

Climber
Summer
□ Prune hard in early spring
7m/23ft
Clematis orientalis
'Sherriffii' *94*
Climber
Summer
□ Prune hard in early spring
7m/23ft
Clematis
'Perle d'Azur' *32, 94, 115*
Climber
Summer
□ Prune in early spring
3m/10ft
Clematis rehderiana *92, 93*
Vigorous climber
Late summer-early autumn
□ Prune in early spring
6m/20ft
Clematis viticella
'Etoile Violette' *57*
Climber
Summer
□ Sun or shade but roots
shaded; rich well-drained soil;
prune early spring
2-3m/6ft 6in-10ft
Convallaria majalis
(lily of the valley) *74, 76*
Rhizomatous perennial
Spring
□ Partial shade; plenty of
leaf-mould
15cm/6in
Convolvulus sabatius, syn.
C. mauritanicus *35, 36*
Trailing perennial
Summer-early autumn
□ Slightly tender
15-20cm/6-8in
Cornus alba
'Elegantissima'
(dogwood) *97, 98*
Deciduous shrub
Spring-early summer
□ Sun or semi-shade; well-
drained soil; prune old stems
back
1.5m/5ft
Cosmos atrosanguineus
(chocolate cosmos) *52, 60*
Tuberous perennial
Late summer
□ Half-hardy; can be
overwintered if protected
60cm/2ft
Crambe maritima
(sea kale) *77, 78*
Perennial
Summer
□ Sun or shade; rich soil
60cm/2ft
Crepis incana
(pink dandelion) *54*
Perennial
Summer
□ Sun or shade
20cm/8in
Crocosmia
'Citronella' (montbretia) *35*
Corm

Late summer
□ Sun and well-drained soil;
divide in spring
60-75cm/2ft-2ft 6in
Crocosmia
'Lucifer' *52, 53*
Corm
Midsummer
□ Sun but not too dry; divide in
spring
up to 1m/3ft 3in
Crocus etruscus
'Zwanenburg' *130*
Corm
Spring
□ Plant 5cm/2in deep
5-10cm/2-4in
Crocus sieberi
'Bowles' White' *57*
Bulb
□ Early-flowering
7.5cm/3in
Crocus sieberi
'Violet Queen' *57*
Corm
Spring
□ Early-flowering
7.5cm/3in
Crocus tommasinianus *38*
Corm
Spring
□ Buds appear in late winter
up to 10cm/4in
Cyclamen coum *57, 114*
Tuber
Winter
□ Semi-shade; well-drained soil
up to 10cm/4in
Cyclamen coum album *97*
Tuber
Winter
□ Semi-shade
up to 10cm/4in

Dahlia
'Bishop of Llandaff' *52*
Tuberous perennial
Summer-autumn
□ Sunny position, rich diet, lift
and replant each year
1m/3ft 3in
Dahlia
'Coltness Hybrids' *133*
Tuberous perennial
Summer-autumn
□ Half-hardy; sunny position;
plant deep or replant annually
45cm/1ft 6in
Daphne retusa *60*
Evergreen shrub
Late spring-early summer
□ Full sun
1.5m/5ft
Delphinium
Belladonna 'Wendy' *94, 115*
Perennial
Summer
□ Sun and rich soil; remove
flower spikes after fading for
second flush
1.1-1.5m/4-5ft
Dianthus barbatus
auricula-eyed

(sweet william) *54, 55*
Biennial
Early summer
□ Sun and good soil
45cm/1ft 6in
Dianthus
'Brympton Red' *54, 56*
Perennial
Summer
□ Sun and well-drained soil;
renew frequently from cuttings
30-45cm/1ft-1ft 6in
Dianthus
'Dad's Favourite' *54*
Perennial
Summer
□ Sun and well-drained soil;
renew frequently
30-45cm/1ft-1ft 6in
Dianthus
'Haytor White' (modern pink)
38, 54
Evergreen perennial
Summer, recurrent
□ Renew frequently from
cuttings
30-45cm/1ft-1ft 6in
Dianthus
'Musgrave's Pink'
(old-fashioned pink) *38*
Evergreen perennial
Summer
□ Renew frequently from
cuttings
30-45cm/1ft-1ft 6in
Dianthus
'Prudence' *118*
Perennial
Summer
□ Sun; alkaline soil
30-45cm/1ft-1ft 6in
Diascia vigilis *60*
Perennial
Summer
□ Tender; sun and rich soil
30-40cm/1ft-1ft 4in
Digitalis lutea
(yellow foxglove) *115, 117*
Perennial
Summer
□ Semi-shade; moist soil
75cm/2ft 6in
Digitalis × mertonensis *115*
Perennial
Summer
□ Semi-shade; moist soil;
divide after flowering
75cm/2ft 6in
Digitalis purpurea alba
(white foxglove) *54, 72, 77,
130*
Perennial or biennial
Summer
□ Semi-shade
1-1.5m/3ft 3in-5ft
Digitalis purpurea
'Sutton's Apricot' *35*
Short lived perennial
Summer
□ Shade
1-1.5m/3ft 3in-5ft
Doronicum plantagineum
'Excelsum' (leopard's bane) *130*

Perennial
Spring
□ Shade
1m/3ft 3in
Dryopteris filix-mas
(male fern) *74*
*Deciduous or semi-evergreen
fern*
Full shade; moist soil
1.2m/4ft

Echium lycopsis
'Blue Bedder', syn.
E. plantagineum (viper's
bugloss) *38*
Annual
Summer
□ Easy
20cm/8in
Elaeagnus × ebbingei
'Limelight' *92*
Evergreen shrub
Autumn
□ Sun or shade; prune to
shape
2m/6ft 6in
Epilobium glabellum
(willow-herb) *57, 59*
Semi-evergreen perennial
All summer
□ Sun or shade
20cm/8in
Eremurus spectabilis
(foxtail lily) *35*
Perennial
Early summer
□ Frost-tender; hard to
establish
1.2m/4ft
Eryngium × oliverianum
(sea holly) *35*
Perennial
Late summer
□ Sun and well-drained soil
60cm-1m/2ft-3ft 3in
Erysimum
'Bowles' Mauve' *32, 33*
Bushy perennial
Spring-summer
□ Half-hardy; renew from
cuttings frequently
up to 75cm/2ft 6in
Erythronium dens-canis
(dog's tooth violet) *57*
Perennial
Spring
□ Semi-shade; rich well-drained
soil; protect tubers from
summer heat
15cm/6in
Escallonia
'Iveyi' *118*
Glossy evergreen shrub
Mid-late summer
□ Tender; trim after flowering
3m/10ft
**Euphorbia amygdaloides
robbiae**
(wood spurge) *97, 98*
Evergreen invasive perennial
Spring
□ Any soil
45-60cm/1ft 6in-2ft

Euphorbia characias wulfenii
(spurge) *77*
Evergreen shrub
Spring
□ Sun or semi-shade
80cm-1m/2ft 8in-3ft 3in
Euphorbia griffithii
'Fireglow' *133, 134*
Perennial
Early summer
□ Sun or shade; moist soil
up to 1m/3ft 3in

Felicia amelloides *34, 38, 115*
Evergreen spreading shrub
Spring-autumn
□ Tender
30-50cm/1ft-1ft 8in
Filipendula vulgaris
'Plena', syn. **F. hexapetala**
'Flore Pleno' (dropwort) *77*
Upright perennial
Summer
□ Sun or semi-shade
1m/3ft 3in
Foeniculum vulgare
(fennel) *94*
Perennial
Summer
□ Sun and well-drained soil; do
not allow to seed
2m/6ft 6in
Foeniculum vulgare
'Purpureum' (bronze fennel) *52*
Perennial
Summer
□ Remove flowerheads after
fading to prevent self-seeding
2m/6ft 6in
Fritillaria imperialis
'Lutea Maxima' *133, 134*
(crown imperial)
Bulb
Spring
□ Sun or semi-shade; rich soil
up to 1.5m/5ft
Fuchsia
'Mme Cornelissen' *54*
Shrub
Summer
□ Tender
up to 1.5m/5ft
Fuchsia
'Riccartonii' *52*
Deciduous shrub
Summer-autumn
□ Sheltered; semi-shade
2m/6ft 6in

Galanthus
'Desdemona' (snowdrop) *74*
Bulb
Winter-early spring
□ Cool soil; divide in spring
10-15cm/4-6in
Galanthus elwesii *74*
Bulb
Winter-early spring
□ Cool soil; divide in spring
15-25cm/6-10in
Galanthus
'Ophelia' *74*
Bulb

Winter-early spring
□ Cool soil; divide in spring
10-15cm/4-6in
Geranium
'Ann Folkard' *115*
Spreading perennial
Summer-autumn
□ Sun
50cm/1ft 8in
Geranium
'Buxton's Blue' *130*
Perennial
Summer-autumn
□ Sun or semi-shade
30cm/1ft
Geranium endressii
'Wargrave Pink' *54*
Perennial
All summer
□ Easy
45cm/1ft 6in
Geranium
'Johnson's Blue' (crane's-bill)
32, 33, 94
Perennial
Early summer
□ Sunny site; cut back after
flowering
30cm/1ft
Geranium macrorrhizum
'Ingwersen's Variety' *112, 114*
Invasive perennial
Late spring-early summer
□ Any soil
50cm/1ft 8in
Geranium
'Russell Prichard' *57*
Semi-evergreen perennial
All summer
□ Easy
30cm/1ft
Geranium sanguineum
'Glenluce' *115*
Perennial
Recurrent
□ Easy
15-20cm/6-8in
Geranium wallichianum
'Buxton's Variety' *35*
Trailing perennial
Midsummer-autumn
□ Any soil
30-45cm/1ft-1ft 6in
Geum
'Mrs Bradshaw' *52*
Perennial
Summer
□Easy
80cm/2ft 8in

Hebe
'La Séduisante' *57*
Evergreen shrub
□ Tender; full sun; cut back in
spring
1m/3ft 3in
Helianthemum
'Ben Hope' (rock rose) *52*
Evergreen
Midsummer
□ Cut back after flowering
23-30cm/9in-1ft
Helichrysum

'Sulphur Light' *115*
Perennial
Mid-late summer
□ Sun and well-drained soil
40-60cm/1ft 4in-2ft
Helleborus foetidus
(hellebore)
'Wester Flisk' (or Miss Jekyll's
scented form) *74, 76*
Perennial
Spring
□ Allow to seed; remove
blotchy leaves
60cm/2ft
Helleborus lividus corsicus *72,
73, 97*
Perennial
Winter-spring
□ Semi-shade; remove leaves
before flowering if mildewed
60cm/2ft
Helleborus orientalis orientalis,
syn. **H. o. olympicus**
(lenten rose) *57, 59*
Evergreen perennial
Winter or early spring
□ Semi-shade; remove diseased
leaves
45cm/1ft 6in
Hemerocallis lilio-asphodelus,
syn. **H. flava** (day lily) *94*
Perennial
Late spring-early summer
□ Full sun; moist soil; divide
annually
60cm/2ft
Hemerocallis
'Marion Vaughn' *130*
Perennial
Midsummer
□ Sun or semi-shade
1m/3ft 3in
Hemerocallis
'Stafford' *52*
Perennial
Mid-late summer
Full sun; moist soil; protect
from slugs and snails in early
spring
75cm/2ft 6in
Hesperis matronalis *60*
(sweet rocket)
Perennial
Summer
□ Sun; any soil; not long-lived
but seeds freely
75cm/2ft 6in
Heuchera
'Apple Blossom' *60*
Perennial
Summer
□ Easy
45-75cm/1ft 6in-2ft 6in
Heuchera micrantha
'Palace Purple' *52*
Perennial
Summer
□ Semi-shade; moist soil
45cm/1ft 6in
Hibiscus syriacus
'Blue Bird' *35*
Deciduous shrub
Late summer-mid autumn

□ Full sun and well-drained soil
3m/10ft
Hosta fortunei albopicta *97, 99*
Perennial
□ Shady site; good soil; protect
from slugs
75cm-1m/2ft 6in-3ft 3in
Hosta fortunei
'Marginata Alba' *77*
Perennial
Midsummer
□ Shade; moist soil
75cm-1m/2ft 6in-3ft 3in
Hosta plantaginea
(August lily) *35, 74*
Clump-forming perennial
Summer
□ Sun; protect from slugs
60cm/2ft
Hosta sieboldiana *72*
Clump-forming perennial
Early summer
□ Shade; protect from slugs
1m/3ft 3in
Humulus lupulus aureus
(golden hop) *115*
Herbaceous twining climber
Summer-autumn
□ Sun or semi-shade
up to 6m/20ft

Iberis sempervirens (candytuft)
133, 135
Evergreen sub-shrub
Late spring-early summer
□ Cut back after flowering
15-30cm/6in-1ft
Iris
'Florentina' *97, 99*
Perennial
Early summer
□ Divide every other year
60cm-1m/2ft-3ft 3in
Iris graminea
(plum tart iris) *57*
Rhizomatous perennial
Late spring
□ Sun or semi-shade; resents
being moved
20-40cm/8in-1ft 4in
Iris
'Jane Phillips' *130*
Rhizomatous perennial
Early summer
□ Divide every other year
70cm-1m/2ft 4in-3ft 3in
Iris pallida pallida, syn.
I. p. dalmatica *32, 34, 35, 38*
Rhizomatous perennial
Summer
□ Sun
70cm-1m/2ft 4in-3ft 3in
Iris pallida
'Variegata' *57, 59*
Rhizomatous perennial
Summer
□ Sun
70cm-1m/2ft 4in-3ft 3in
Iris sibirica
'Splash Down' *94*
Rhizomatous perennial
Late spring-early summer
□ Easy

1m/3ft 3in
Itea ilicifolia *74, 76*
Evergreen bushy shrub
Late summer-early autumn
□ Sun or semi-shade; moist soil
3m/10ft

Jasminum nudiflorum
(winter-flowering jasmine) *92*
Deciduous cascading climber
Early spring
□ Full sun; shear old shoots
after flowering
3m/10ft

Knautia macedonica *52*
Perennial
Summer
□ Sunny place; may need
support
75cm/2ft 6in
Kniphofia caulescens
(red-hot poker) *52*
Evergreen perennial
Autumn
□ Tender; full sun and well-
drained soil
1.2m/4ft

Lathyrus latifolius
(perennial pea) *57*
Herbaceous climber
Summer-autumn
□ Dead-head regularly
2m/6ft 6in
Lavatera olbia
'Barnsley' (tree mallow) *60, 61*
Semi-evergreen shrub
All summer
□ Sun; do not allow to revert
1.5m/5ft
Lavatera olbia
'Burgundy Wine' *118*
Deciduous shrub
Recurrent
□ Prune in spring
1.5m/5ft
Leucojum aestivum
'Gravetye Giant' (snowflake) *74*
Bulb
Early spring
□ Cool soil; divide in spring
10-15cm/4in-6in
Ligustrum lucidum
(Chinese privet) *74*
Evergreen shrub or tree
Late summer-early autumn
□ Sun or semi-shade
10m/33ft
Lilium candidum
(madonna lily) *77*
Bulb
Summer
□ Limy soil; sun
1-2m/3ft 3in-6ft 6in
Lilium martagon album
(turk's-cap lily) *97*
Bulb
Summer
□ Shade and leaf-mould
1-2m/3ft 3in-6ft 6in
Lilium regale
(regal lily) *54, 56, 60, 77, 130*

Bulb
Summer
□ Prone to lily beetle
50cm-2m/1ft 8in-6ft 6in
Limnanthes douglasii
(poached egg flower) *35*
Annual
Early-late summer
□ Sun; self-seeder
15cm/6in
Linum perenne (flax) *32*
Perennial
Summer
□ Sun; well-drained; peaty soil
30cm/1ft
Lonicera × brownii
'Dropmore Scarlet'
(honeysuckle) *52*
Deciduous climber
All summer
□ Tender; prune after flowering
4m/13ft
Lonicera japonica
'Halliana' (honeysuckle) *74*
Deciduous climber
Summer
□ Slightly tender
up to 5m/16ft 6in
Lonicera periclymenum
'Graham Thomas'
(honeysuckle) *92*
Deciduous, woody climber
Summer
□ Prune old wood after
flowering
7m/23ft
Lunaria annua
(honesty) *32*
Biennial
Spring-early summer
□ Partial shade; self-seeder
75cm/2ft 6in
Lunaria annua variegata alba
(white variegated honesty) *57,
77*
Biennial
Spring-early summer
□ Semi-shade; self-seeder
75cm/2ft 6in
Lychnis coronaria alba
(campion) *118*
Short-lived perennial
Summer
□ Sun; self-seeder
45-60cm/1ft 6in-2ft
Lysimachia clethroides
(loosestrife) *97, 99*
Perennial
Late summer
□ Sun; moist soil
1m/3ft 3in
Lysimachia ephemerum *77,
130*
Perennial
Recurrent
□ Sun or semi-shade
1m/3ft 3in

Magnolia salicifolia *77*
Deciduous tree
Mid spring
□ Sun and shelter; neutral or
acid soil

10cm/4in
Malus domestica
'Discovery' (apple tree) *133, 135*
Fruit tree
Spring, autumn
□ Good soil; prune in summer
once established
Height according to variety
Malva
'Primley Blue' *130, 132*
Low climber
All summer
□ Renew from cuttings
up to 1m/3ft 3in
Melianthus major
(honey bush) *94*
Evergreen shrub
Spring-summer
□ Tender; sun and well-drained
soil
2-3m/6ft 6in-10ft
Mimulus aurantiacus
(monkey flower) *35*
Evergreen shrub
Late spring-autumn
□ Tender
70cm/2ft 4in
Morina longifolia
(whorl flower) *60*
Evergreen perennial
Midsummer
□ Full sun
60-75cm/2ft-2ft 6in
Myosotis alpestris
(forget-me-not) *115*
Hardy perennial
Spring-summer
□ Best treated as a biennial
20-25cm/8-10in
Myosotis
'Blue Ball' *38, 115*
Short-lived perennial
Spring-summer
□ Renew each year
10-15cm/4-6in
Myosotis
'White Ball' *115*
Short-lived perennial
Spring-summer
□ Renew each year
up to 20cm/8in
Myrrhis odorata
(sweet cicely) *74, 76*
Perennial herb
Early summer
□ Sun or shade; prevent from
seeding
60cm/2ft

Narcissus
'February Gold' *130*
Bulb
Early spring
□ Sun or light shade
32cm/13in
Narcissus
'February Silver' *92*
Bulb
Early spring
□ Sun or light shade
32cm/13in
Narcissus
'Silver Chimes' *130*

Bulb
Mid-late spring
□ Sun or light shade
32cm/13in
Narcissus
'Tête-à-Tête' *133, 135*
Bulb
Early spring
□ Sun or light shade
15-30cm/6in-1ft
Narcissus
'Thalia' *32, 97*
Bulb
Mid spring
38cm/15in
Narcissus
'W.P. Milner' *35*
Bulb
Early spring
□ Sun or partial shade
23cm/9in
Nectaroscordum siculum,
syn. **Allium siculum** *35, 37*
Bulb
Late spring-early summer,
□ Sun; well-drained soil
3m/10ft
Nemophila menziesii, syn.
N. insignis
(baby blue-eyes) *38*
Annual
Summer
□ Sun or semi-shade
20cm/8in
Nepeta
'Six Hills Giant' (catmint) *35, 36*
Perennial
Early-late summer
□ Well-drained soil; divide
often
60cm-1m/2ft-3ft 3in
Nicotiana langsdorfii
(tobacco plant) *72, 115*
Perennial
Summer
□ Half-hardy
1-1.5m/3ft 3in-5ft
Nicotiana sylvestris
(flowering tobacco) *130*
Perennial
Late summer
□ Tender; sun or shade
1.5m/5ft
Nigella damascena
'Miss Jekyll' (love-in-a-mist) *38*
Annual
Summer
□ Easy
45cm/1ft 6in

Oenothera tetragona
(evening primrose) *92, 94*
Perennial
Mid-late summer
□ Easy
30-90cm/1-3ft
Olearia × scilloniensis *77*
Evergreen shrub
Late spring
□ Tender
2m/6ft 6in
Omphalodes cappadocica
(navelwort) *130, 132*

Perennial
Spring-summer
□ Shade; moist soil
15-20cm/6-8in
Onopordum acanthium
(Scotch thistle) *35, 77*
Biennial
Summer
□ Sun or semi-shade; well-
drained soil; remove heads to
prevent self-seeding
1.8m/6ft
Origanum vulgare aureum
(golden marjoram) *92*
Perennial herb
Summer
□ Semi-shade, will scorch in
full sun
8cm/3in
Osmanthus delavayi *57*
Evergreen bushy shrub
Mid-late spring
□ Sun or shade; cut back after
flowering
3.5m/11ft 6in
Osteospermum barberae
'Blue Streak', syn.
Dimorphotheca barberae
(cape marigold) *115*
Perennial
Late summer
□ Frost-hardy; sun and well-
drained soil
30cm/1ft
Osteospermum ecklonis, syn.
Dimorphotheca ecklonis *54*
Evergreen perennial
Summer-autumn
□ Half-hardy
45cm/1ft 6in

Paeonia lactiflora
'Félix Crousse' (peony) *112, 114*
Perennial
Summer
□ Sun or light shade; rich soil
75cm/2ft 6in
Paeonia lactiflora
'Instituteur Doriat' *112*
Perennial
Summer
□ Sun or light shade; rich soil
1m/3ft 3in
Paeonia mlokosewitschii *94*
Perennial
Late spring-early summer
□ Sun or light shade; rich,
well-drained soil
75cm/2ft 6in
Paeonia officinalis
'Rubra Plena' *54, 56*
Perennial
Spring-early summer
□ Sun or shade; easy
75cm/2ft 6in
Papaver nudicaule *135*
(Iceland poppy)
Perennial
Summer
□ Sun or shade
up to 30cm/1ft
Penstemon
'Apple Blossom' *115, 117*

Semi-evergreen perennial
Midsummer
□ Sun and well-drained soil;
renew from cuttings annually
45cm/1ft 6in
Penstemon
'Garnet' *54, 56, 60, 118*
Semi-evergreen perennial
Midsummer-autumn
□ Tender; renew from cuttings
60-75cm/2ft-2ft 6in
Penstemon
'Sour Grapes' *118*
Perennial
Recurrent
□ Renew from cuttings each
year
60cm/2ft
Perovskia atriplicifolia *115, 118*
Deciduous sub-shrub
Late summer-mid autumn
□ Sun and light soil; prune in
spring
1.2m/5ft
Petroselinum crispum
(parsley) *54*
Perennial
Short-lived; do not allow to
seed
□ Cool, rich soil
25cm/10in
Phacelia campanularia
(California bluebell) *38*
Bushy annual
Summer and early autumn
□ Easy and fast
20cm/8in
Philadelphus coronarius
'Aureus'
(mock orange) *97*
Deciduous shrub
Late spring-early summer
□ Shade
2.5m/8ft
Phlox maculata
'Omega' *57*
Perennial
Summer
Moist soil; divide in early
spring
1m/3ft 3in
Phygelius aequalis
'Indian Chief' *52*
Sub-shrub
Summer
□ Tender; sun and sheltered site
1m/3ft 3in
Phygelius aequalis
'Yellow Trumpet' *92*
Evergreen sub-shrub
Recurrent
□ Tender; cut back to live
wood in spring
1m/3ft 3in
Phyllitis scolopendrium,
syn. **Asplenium scolopendrium**
(hart's-tongue fern) *74, 76*
Evergreen fern
□ Shade
45-75cm/1ft 6in-2ft 6in
Polemonium caeruleum
(Jacob's ladder) *94, 96*
Perennial

Early summer
□ Easy self-seeder
45-60cm/1ft 6in-2ft
Polygonum amplexicaule *52*
Perennial
Summer-autumn
□ Sun or shade; moist soil
1.2m/4ft
Polystichum setiferum
(soft shield fern) *72, 74*
Evergreen fern
□ Shade; moist soil
60cm/2ft
Potentilla atrosanguinea
(cinquefoil) *52*
Clump-forming perennial
Mid-late summer
□ Sun; well-drained soil
30-50cm/1ft-1ft 8in
Potentilla nepalensis
'Miss Willmott' *60*
Clump-forming perennial
Summer
□ Divide occasionally
50cm/1ft 8in
Primula vulgaris
'Alba Plena' (double white
primrose) *112*
Perennial
Spring
□ Moist soil; divide annually
15-20cm/6-8in
Primula
'Wanda' *112, 114*
Perennial
Spring
□ Moist soil; divide annually
15-20cm/6-8in
Prunus laurocerasus
'Otto Luyken' (cherry laurel)
72
Evergreen shrub
Late spring
□ Easy; shade-tolerant
75cm-1m/2ft 6in-3ft 3in
Prunus mume
'Omoi-no-mama'
(Japanese apricot) *130, 132*
Deciduous shrub
Early spring
□ Sun and well-drained soil;
best against a wall
2m/6ft 6in
Prunus tenella
'Fire Hill' *54*
Deciduous shrub
Mid-late spring
□ Prune after flowering
2m/6ft 6in
Pyracantha
'Watereri' (firethorn) *112*
Evergreen shrub
Early summer
□ Sheltered site; sun or semi-
shade; fertile soil
2.5m/8ft
Pyrus calleryana
'Chanticleer' *77*
Deciduous tree
Spring
□ Strong-growing and resistant
to fireblight
10m/33ft

Rhodochiton atrosanguineum
52
Evergreen climber
Late spring-late autumn
□ Frost-tender
3m/10ft
Ribes laurifolium
(winter-flowering currant) *130*
Evergreen shrub
Late winter-early spring
□ Prune in early spring
75cm-1m/2ft 6in-3ft 3in
Ribes speciosum
(fuchsia-flowered currant) *52*
Spiny shrub
Mid-late spring
□ Warm site; prune in early
spring
2m/6ft 6in
Romneya coulteri
(California tree poppy) *32*
Sub-shrubby perennial
Late summer
□ Sunny site; can be invasive
2m/6ft 6in
Rosa
'Albéric Barbier' *32*
Semi-evergreen rambler
Summer, recurrent
□ Sun or shade
up to 5m/16ft 6in
Rosa
'Alchymist' *35, 36*
Climbing rose
Late spring-early summer
□ Prune in spring
3.5m/11ft 6in
Rosa
'Alister Stella Gray' *94*
Noisette climber
Summer-autumn
□ Prune in spring
5m/16ft 6in
Rosa chinensis
'Mutabilis' *52*
Bush rose
Summer-autumn
□ Sunny, sheltered wall
1m/3ft 3in
Rosa
'De Rescht' *60*
Damask rose
Summer, recurrent
□ Prune in spring
90cm/3ft
Rosa
'Dupontii' (snowbush rose) *77*
Bushy shrub rose
Midsummer
□ Prune out old wood
2.2m/7ft
Rosa
'Ferdinand Pichard' *54, 56*
Hybrid perpetual rose
Summer-autumn
□ Rich soil
1.5m/5ft
Rosa
'Frau Dagmar Hastrup' *112, 113*
Rugosa rose
Late summer-autumn
□ Thin out old wood
1m/3ft 3in

Rosa
'Gloire de Dijon' *35*
Climbing rose
Summer-autumn
□ Warm wall
4m/13ft
Rosa
'Golden Wings' *92, 97*
Spreading shrub rose
Summer-autumn
□ Prune old wood
1.1m/3ft 8in
Rosa hugonis
(golden rose of China) *94, 96*
Shrub rose
Early summer
□ Prune dead and oldest wood
only
2.5m/8ft
Rosa
'Mermaid' *92*
Evergreen climbing rose
Recurrent
□ Sheltered wall
up to 6m/20ft
Rosa
'Mme Alfred Carrière' *57, 72*
Climber
Summer-autumn
□ Vigorous and recurrent
up to 5.5m/18ft
Rosa
'Mme Grégoire Staechelin' *60*
Climbing rose
Summer
□ Spring prune
6m/20ft
Rosa
'Mme Isaac Pereire' *118*
Bourbon rose
Summer-autumn
□ Rich soil
2.2m/7ft
Rosa moyesii *52*
Strong-growing shrub rose
Summer
□ Prune out old branches
4m/13ft
Rosa
'Nathalie Nypels' *115*
Floribunda rose
Summer
□ Spring prune
90cm/3ft
Rosa nutkana
'Plena', syn. **R. californica**
'Plena' *57*
Shrub rose
Summer
□ Prune in spring occasionally
2m/6ft 6in
Rosa
'Pearl Drift' *35*
Shrub rose
Summer-autumn
□ Dead-head to keep flowering
1.5m/5ft
Rosa
'The Fairy' *54, 56*
Bush rose
Late summer-autumn
□ Prune lightly
60cm/2ft

Rosa·
'Tynwald' *94*
Bush rose
Summer
□ Prune in spring
1m/3ft 3in
Rosa
'Yvonne Rabier' *72*
Polyantha bush rose
Summer-autumn
□ Prune lightly
45cm/1ft 6in
Rosmarinus officinalis
'Miss Jessopp's Upright'
(rosemary) *38*
Evergreen, upright shrub
Mid-late spring and sometimes
again in autumn
□ Sun and well-drained soil;
prune after flowering
2m/6ft 6in
Rosmarinus officinalis
'Severn Sea' *32*
Evergreen shrub
Mid-late spring
□ Sunny, well-drained site;
trim after flowering
1m/3ft 3in
Rubus cockburnianus *112*
Deciduous arching shrub
Early summer, winter
□ Cut back late summer
2.5m/8ft
Ruta graveolens
'Jackman's Blue' (rue) *130*
Evergreen sub-shrub
Summer
□ Sun and well-drained soil; cut
back in spring
75cm/2ft 6in

Salix hastata
'Wehrhahnii' *112*
Deciduous shrub
Early spring
□ Moist soil, prune old stems
75cm/2ft 6in
Salpiglossis sinuata
'Splash' *133*
Annual
Summer-early autumn
□ Half-hardy
60cm/2ft
Salvia involucrata
'Bethellii' *60, 61*
Sub-shrub
Late summer-autumn
□ Tender; renew from
cuttings
1.2-1.5m/4-5ft
Salvia microphylla neurepia
(scarlet sage) *54*
Shrub
Summer-autumn
□ Half-hardy, sun and well-
drained soil
1m/3ft 3in
Salvia officinalis
'Purpurascens' (purple sage) *52*
Semi-evergreen herb
Summer
□ Tender, renew every 3 years
60cm/2ft

Salvia patens
'Cambridge Blue' *94*
Perennial
Summer-autumn
□ Half-hardy, can be lifted and
stored
45-60cm/1ft 6in-2ft
Salvia sclarea turkestanica *115*
Biennial
Summer
□ Sun, self-seeder
75cm/2ft 6in
Salvia × superba
'May Night' *115*
Perennial
Summer
□ Sun; well-drained soil
1m/3ft 3in
Sambucus racemosa
'Plumosa Aurea' (cut-leaf elder)
97, 98
Deciduous shrub
Midsummer
□ Shady position; sun will
scorch leaves
3m/10ft
Santolina pinnata neapolitana
92
Evergreen shrub
Midsummer
□ Cut back in spring
75cm/2ft 6in
Saponaria officinalis
'Rosea Plena' (soapwort) *54*
Invasive perennial
Summer
□ Easy
60-90cm/2-3ft
Sarcococca hookeriana digyna
(Christmas box) *74, 77*
Evergreen shrub
Winter-spring
□ Shade
1.5m/5ft
Saxifraga × urbium
(London pride) *57, 74*
Evergreen perennial
Summer
□ Moist soil
30cm/1ft
Scilla siberica
'Spring Beauty' *32, 38*
Bulb
Early spring
□ Sunny; well-drained soil
5cm/2in
Sedum spectabile
(ice plant) *60*
Perennial
Late summer
□ Dry soil
45cm/1ft 6in
Sidalcea
'Loveliness' *54*
Perennial
Summer
□ Sun and well-drained soil;
divide in spring
1m/3ft 3in
Silybum marianum
(milk thistle) *77, 118*
Biennial
Summer-early autumn

□ Sun; well-drained soil
1.2m/4ft
Sisyrinchium striatum *92*
Semi-evergreen perennial
Summer
□ Any soil
45-60cm/1ft 6in-2ft
Solanum crispum
'Glasnevin' (Chilean potato
tree) *118*
Semi-evergreen, lax climber
Summer
□ Tender; full sun; thin out in
spring
up to 6m/20ft
Solanum jasminoides
'Album' *57, 59*
Semi-evergreen climber
Summer-autumn
□ Half-hardy; full sun; grow
on a wall; thin out in spring
up to 6m/20ft
Spartium junceum
(Spanish broom) *130, 132*
Deciduous shrub
Early summer-early autumn
□ Tender; sun; poor soil; clip in
early spring
3m/10ft
Stachys byzantina, syn.
S. olympica *36, 60*
Semi-evergreen perennial
□ Well-drained soil; remove
withered leaves regularly
45cm/1ft 6in
Stachys byzantina
'Silver Carpet' *35*
*Evergreen, mat-forming
perennial*
□ Easy
15cm/6in

Tanacetum parthenium
(golden feverfew) *130*
Perennial
Summer
□ Sunny, well-drained position
30-60cm/1ft-2ft
Teucrium fruticans
(tree germander) *35*
Shrub
Summer
□ Best against a warm wall
2m/6ft 6in
Thalictrum aquilegifolium
'White Cloud' (meadow rue) *57*
Perennial

Summer
□ Sun or light shade
1-1.2m/3ft 3in-4ft
Thalictrum flavum *94*
Perennial
Mid-late summer
□ Sun or light shade; not too
dry
1.2-1.5m/4-5ft
Tropaeolum majus
'Empress of India' (nasturtium)
52
Annual
Summer
□ Easy; half-hardy
25cm/10in
Tulipa acuminata
(tulip) *133*
Bulb
Mid spring
□ Sun or shade; plant deep or
renew each year
30-45cm/1ft-1ft 6in
Tulipa
'Angélique' *60, 118*
Bulb
Late spring
□ Sun or shade; plant deep or
renew each year
40cm/1ft 4in
Tulipa
'Bellona' *94*
Bulb
Early
□ Sun or shade; plant deep or
lift and replant each year
30cm/1ft
Tulipa clusiana
(lady tulip) *115, 118*
Bulb
Mid spring
□ Sun or shade; plant deep;
renew each year
up to 25cm/10in
Tulipa
'Estella Rijnveld' *118*
Bulb
Late spring
□ Sun or shade; plant deep or
renew each year
45cm/1ft 6in
Tulipa
'Generaal de Wet' *52*
Bulb
Early spring
□ Plant deep or renew each year
45cm/1ft 6in

Tulipa
'Palestrina' *115*
Bulb
Late spring
□ Sun or shade; plant deep or
renew each year
45cm/1ft 6in
Tulipa praestans *52*
Bulb
Early spring
□ Plant deep or renew each year
10-45cm/4in-1ft 6in
Tulipa
'Purissima' *35, 77*
Bulb
Early-mid spring
□ Plant deep or renew each
year
35-40cm/1ft 2in-1ft 4in
Tulipa
'Queen of Night' *32, 57, 59*
Bulb
Late spring
□ Sunny; light soil; plant deep
or renew each year
60cm/2ft
Tulipa
'Schoonoord' *38*
Bulb
Spring
□ Sunny; light soil; plant deep
or renew each year
60cm/2ft
Tulipa
'Shirley' *57, 60*
Bulb
Spring
□ Plant deep or renew each year
60cm/2ft
Tulipa
'Spring Green' *72*
Bulb
Late spring
□ Sun or shade; plant deep or
lift and replant each year
60cm/2ft
Tulipa sylvestris *92*
Bulb
Early spring
□ Sun or shade; light soil
10-45cm/4in-1ft 6in
Tulipa
'Texas Gold' (yellow parrot) *92*
Bulb
Early spring
□ Plant deep or renew each year
60cm/2ft

Tulipa
'West Point' *94, 96*
Bulb
Late spring
□ Sun or shade; plant deep or
lift and replant each year
50cm/1ft 8in
Tulipa
'White Triumphator' *72, 73*
Bulb
Late spring
□ Sun or shade; plant deep or
lift and replant each year
65-70cm/2ft-2ft 3in

Valeriana phu
'Aurea' *130*
Perennial
Summer
□ Sunny; well-drained soil
38cm/1ft
Veratrum album
(white false hellebore) *97, 98*
Perennial
Summer
□ Semi-shade; divide in autumn
2m/6ft 6in
Verbascum olympicum
(mullein) *92*
Biennial or short-lived perennial
Midsummer
□ Sun
2m/6ft 6in
Verbena bonariensis *32*
Perennial
Summer-autumn
□ Tender; sunny, well-drained
site
2m/6ft 6in
Verbena
'Silver Anne' *54*
Perennial
Summer
□ Tender
15cm/6in
Verbena
'Sissinghurst' *118*
Perennial
Summer
□ Half-hardy; sun and well-
drained soil
15-20cm/6-8in
Veronica
'Blue Fountain' *38, 39*
Perennial
Midsummer-autumn
□ Well-drained, sunny position

25cm/10in
Viburnum carlesii
'Diana' *112, 114*
Deciduous shrub
Mid-late spring
□ Sun or semi-shade; moist
soil; thin out older shoots after
flowering
2m/6ft 6in
Viburnum tinus
'Eve Price' *72*
Evergreen shrub
Winter-spring
□ Dry soil
3m/10ft
Viola
'Aspasia' *92*
Perennial
Midsummer, recurrent
□ Cut back hard and water to
encourage flowering
25cm/10in
Viola
'Boughton Blue' *38*
Perennial
Early-midsummer
□ Cut down as flowers start to
dwindle
45cm/1ft 6in
Viola cornuta alba *54, 77, 92*
Perennial
Spring and summer
□ Sun or shade; cut back as
flowers divide
12-20cm/5-8in
Viola
'Huntercombe Purple' *32, 34,
57*
Perennial
Spring-late summer
□ Sunny, well-drained site
15-30cm/6in-1ft
Vitis vinifera
'Purpurea' (grapevine) *52*
Deciduous climber
Summer
□ Rich soil and sun; prune hard
in late autumn
7m/23ft

Weigela
'Florida Variegata' *115*
Deciduous shrub
Late spring
□ Sunny fertile soil; prune out
branches after flowering
1.5m/5ft

COLOUR DIRECTORY

The following lists of plants are arranged in colour sequences. Where leaf or berry colour dominates they are listed under that shade, rather than in the group to which their less significant flowers belong. Some plants which have as much leaf or berry colour as flower will appear in two lists. Names followed by an asterisk do not appear in any of the plans in this book, but are plants which I have grown and enjoyed and would have included had there been space.

BLUE SPECTRUM

Pale blues
Amsonia tabernaemontana*
Campanula lactiflora*
Campanula persicifolia 'Telham Beauty'*
Chionodoxa luciliae
Iris pallida
Lobelia 'Cambridge Blue'*
Muscari tubergenianum*
Nemophila menziesii
Nierembergia repens*
Platycodon grandiflorum*
Rosmarinus officinalis 'Severn Sea'
Salvia patens 'Cambridge Blue'*
Scabiosa caucasica 'Clive Greaves'*
Teucrium fruticans
Veronica gentianoides*

True blues
Agapanthus 'Headbourne Hybrids'
Anchusa azurea 'Loddon Royalist'*
Anchusa capensis 'Blue Angel'*
Anemone blanda 'Atrocaerulea'
Aquilegia alpina
Brunnera macrophylla*
Ceanothus 'Autumnal Blue'
Ceanothus 'Burkwoodii'
Ceanothus 'Cascade'
Ceanothus impressus
Ceratostigma plumbaginoides
Ceratostigma willmottianum
Clematis alpina 'Frances Rivis'
Clematis 'Perle d'Azur'
Delphinium Belladonna 'Blue Bees'*
Delphinium Belladonna 'Wendy'
Echium lycopsis 'Blue Bedder'*
Felicia amelloides
Gentiana acaulis*
Geranium 'Johnson's Blue'

Geranium wallichianum 'Buxton's Variety'
Ipomoea 'Heavenly Blue'*
Iris 'Jane Phillips'
Iris reticulata 'Joyce'*
Iris sibirica 'Splash Down'
Linum narbonense*
Linum perenne
Meconopsis × sheldonii*
Myosotis 'Blue Ball'
Nigella damascena 'Miss Jekyll'
Phacelia campanularia
Salvia patens*
Scilla siberica 'Spring Beauty'
Veronica 'Blue Fountain'
Viola 'Boughton Blue'
Viola 'Ullswater'*

Blue mauves
Abutilon vitifolium 'Veronica Tennant'
Aster × frikartii 'Mönch'*
Aster × thompsonii 'Nanus'
Buddleja 'Lochinch'
Camassia cusickii
Camassia leichtlinii*
Campanula lactiflora 'Prichard's Variety'*
Clematis 'Mrs Cholmondeley'
Convolvulus sabatius
Crocus etruscus 'Zwanenburg'
Crocus 'Queen of the Blues'*
Crocus tommasinianus
Eryngium × oliverianum
Galega officinalis*
Hibiscus syriacus 'Blue Bird'
Lavandula angustifolia*
Malva 'Primley Blue'
Nepeta 'Six Hills Giant'
Penstemon 'Sour Grapes'
Perovskia atriplicifolia
Phlox 'Chattahoochee'*
Phlox paniculata 'Fairy's Petticoat'*
Polemonium caeruleum
Pulmonaria angustifolia 'Munstead Blue'*
Rosmarinus officinalis 'Miss Jessopp's Upright'
Solanum crispum 'Glasnevin'
Syringa vulgaris 'Firmament'*
Thalictrum aquilegifolium*
Vinca minor 'La Grave'*
Wisteria floribunda*

Pink mauves
Campanula lactiflora 'Loddon Anna' *
Clematis 'Comtesse de Bouchaud'*
Clematis 'Lady Betty Balfour'*
Clematis 'Nelly Moser'*
Dictamnus fraxinella*
Hesperis matronalis
Linaria purpurea 'Canon Went'*
Polemonium foliosissimum*
Pulsatilla vulgaris*
Syringa palibiniana*

RED SPECTRUM

Pale pinks
Abelia × grandiflora
Actinidia kolomikta
Aquilegia vulgaris
Aster lateriflorus 'Horizontalis'
Clematis montana 'Elizabeth'
Cleome 'Pink Queen'*
Crepis incana
Dianthus barbatus auricula-eyed*
Dianthus 'Emile Paré'*
Diascia vigilis
Erigeron mucronatus*
Escallonia 'Apple Blossom'*
Geranium macrorrhizum 'Ingwersen's Variety'
Geranium sanguineum 'Glenluce'
Helleborus orientalis orientalis
Heuchera 'Apple Blossom'
Lavatera olbia 'Barnsley'
Malus domestica 'Discovery'
Malus 'Katherine'*
Morina longifolia
Penstemon 'Apple Blossom'
Penstemon 'Evelyn'*
Prunus mume 'Omoi-no-mama'
Rosa 'Frau Dagmar Hastrup'
Rosa 'Mme Pierre Oger'*
Salvia sclarea turkestanica
Saponaria officinalis 'Rosea Plena'
Saxifraga × urbium
Sidalcea 'Loveliness'
Syringa microphylla*
Verbena 'Silver Anne'
Viburnum carlesii 'Diana'
Weigela 'Florida Variegata'

Strong pinks
Aster novae-angliae 'Harrington's Pink'*
Bergenia 'Ballawley'*
Camellia 'Donation'*
Cercis siliquastrum*
Cistus × purpureus*
Cyclamen coum
Daphne retusa
Dicentra 'Adrian Bloom'*
Geranium cinereum 'Ballerina'*
Geranium 'Russell Prichard'
Lathyrus latifolius
Potentilla nepalensis 'Miss Willmott'
Prunus tenella 'Fire Hill'
Rosa 'Constance Spry'*
Rosa 'Fritz Nobis'*
Rosa 'Mme Grégoire Staechelin'
Rosa nutkana 'Plena'
Salvia involucrata 'Bethellii'
Sedum spectabile
Tulipa 'Angélique'
Verbena 'Sissinghurst'
Viburnum × bodnantense*

Traces of salmon pink
Dianthus 'Doris'*
Digitalis × mertonensis

Geranium endressii 'Wargrave Pink'
Papaver orientale 'Mrs Perry'*
Rosa 'The Fairy'

Scarlet reds
Acer palmatum coreanum*
Chaenomeles superba 'Rowallane'*
Cheiranthus cheiri 'Vulcan'
Crocosmia 'Lucifer'
Dahlia 'Bishop of Llandaff'
Dahlia 'Coltness Hybrids'
Fritillaria imperialis
Fuchsia 'Riccartonii'
Geum 'Mrs Bradshaw'
Helianthemum 'Ben Hope'
Hemerocallis 'Stafford'
Heuchera 'Red Spangles'*
Lobelia cardinalis*
Lonicera × brownii 'Dropmore Scarlet'
Malus 'John Downie'*
Monarda didyma 'Cambridge Scarlet'
Paeonia tenuifolia*
Papaver orientale 'Indian Chief'*
Phlox paniculata 'Starfire'*
Phygelius aequalis 'Indian Chief'
Polygonum amplexicaule
Potentilla atrosanguinea*
Potentilla 'Red Ace'*
Primula 'Red Hugh'*
Pyracantha 'Watereri'
Ribes speciosum
Rosa 'Alec's Red'*
Rosa 'Frau Dagmar Hastrup'
Rosa moyesii
Rosa 'Scarlet Fire'*
Salpiglossis sinuata 'Splash'
Salvia microphylla neurepia
Tropaeolum 'Empress of India'
Tropaeolum speciosum*
Tulipa praestans

Crimson reds
Antirrhinum 'Crimson Monarch'
Centranthus ruber
Clematis 'Gravetye Beauty'*
Clematis 'Kermesina'*
Dianthus barbatus auricula-eyed*
Dianthus 'Brympton Red'
Dianthus 'Prudence'*
Fuchsia 'Mme Cornelissen'
Linum grandiflorum rubrum*
Lychnis coronaria*
Malus 'Lemoinei'*
Malus sargentii*
Paeonia lactiflora 'Félix Crousse'
Paeonia lactiflora 'Instituteur Doriat'
Paeonia officinalis 'Rubra Plena'
Penstemon 'Garnet'
Rosa 'De Rescht'
Rosa 'Ferdinand Pichard'
Tulipa clusiana
Tulipa 'Estella Rijnveld'

Strong purples
Abutilon × suntense

Acanthus balcanicus
Acanthus spinosus
Buddleja davidii 'Black Knight'
Clematis 'Jackmanii Superba'
Clematis viticella 'Etoile Violette'
Crocus sieberi 'Violet Queen'
Daphne mezereum*
Erysimum 'Bowles' Mauve'
Fuchsia 'Riccartonii'
Geranium 'Ann Folkard'
Gladiolus byzantinus*
Hebe 'La Séduisante'
Heliotropium 'Princess Marina'*
Helleborus orientalis orientalis
Iris graminea
Lathyrus latifolius
Lavandula angustifolia 'Hidcote'*
Lunaria annua
Magnolia liliiflora 'Nigra'*
Origanum laevigatum*
Primula 'Wanda'
Rosa 'Cerise Bouquet'*
Rosa 'Mme Isaac Pereire'
Salvia 'Victoria'*
Syringa vulgaris 'Souvenir de Louis
  Spaeth'*
Verbena bonariensis
Viola 'Huntercombe Purple'

Maroons and black purples
Alcea rosea 'Nigra'
Cosmos atrosanguineus
Dianthus 'Dad's Favourite'
Fritillaria pyrenaica*
Helleborus atrorubens*
Knautia macedonica
Lavatera olbia 'Burgundy Wine'
Rosa 'Guinée'*
Rosa 'Tuscany'*
Rhodochiton atrosanguineum
Sedum maximum atropurpureum*
Tulipa 'Queen of Night'
Viola labradorica*

YELLOW SPECTRUM

Clear or pale yellows
Achillea 'Moonshine'
Aconitum vulparia
Alcea rugosa
Alyssum 'Citrinum'*
Argyranthemum maderense
Cephalaria gigantea
Cheiranthus cheiri 'Moonlight'
Cheiranthus 'Primrose Bedder'*
Clematis rehderiana
Corylopsis pauciflora*
Cytisus kewensis*
Digitalis lutea
Elaeagnus × ebbingei 'Limelight'
Eremurus spectabilis
Erythronium 'Pagoda'*
Forsythia suspensa*
Helichrysum 'Sulphur Light'
Hemerocallis lilio-asphodelus

Hemerocallis 'Marion Vaughn'
Hypericum olympicum 'Citrinum'*
Limnanthes douglasii
Lonicera japonica 'Halliana'
Lonicera periclymenum 'Graham
  Thomas'
Lupinus arboreus*
Narcissus 'February Silver'
Narcissus 'W.P. Milner'
Nepeta govaniana*
Paeonia mlokosewitschii
Papaver nudicaule*
Phygelius aequalis 'Yellow Trumpet'
Potentilla 'Vilmoriniana'*
Primula vulgaris*
Rhododendron lutescens*
Rosa 'Albéric Barbier'
Rosa 'Alister Stella Gray'
Rosa banksiae 'Lutea'*
Rosa hugonis
Rosa 'Mermaid'
Santolina pinnata 'Sulphurea'*
Syringa vulgaris 'Primrose'*
Thalictrum flavum
Tulipa sylvestris
Tulipa 'West Point'
Verbascum elegantissimum
  'Gainsborough'*
Verbascum olympicum
Viola 'Aspasia'

Gold yellows
Acacia dealbata
Azara microphylla
Cheiranthus cheiri 'Harpur Crewe'*
Clematis orientalis 'Bill Mackenzie'
Crocosmia 'Citronella'
Cytisus battandieri
Dahlia 'Coltness Hybrids'
Doronicum plantagineum 'Excelsum'
Foeniculum vulgare
Fritillaria imperialis 'Aurora'*
Genista aetnensis*
Jasminum nudiflorum
Laburnum watereri 'Vossii'*
Malus 'Golden Hornet'*
Narcissus 'February Gold'
Narcissus 'Tête-à-Tête'
Oenothera tetragona
Origanum vulgare aureum
Paeonia lutea 'Ludlowii'*
Philadelphus coronarius 'Aureus'
Piptanthus nepalensis*
Rosa 'Golden Showers'*
Rosa 'Golden Wings'
Rudbeckia hirta 'Rustic Dwarfs'*
Spartium junceum
Tulipa 'Bellona'
Tulipa 'Texas Gold'
Viburnum opulus 'Xanthocarpum'*

Oranges and apricots
Calendula officinalis
Cheiranthus cheiri 'Wenlock Beauty'
Chrysanthemum carinatum
  'Monarch Court Jesters'

Crocosmia × crocosmiiflora*
Digitalis purpurea 'Sutton's Apricot'
Euphorbia griffithii 'Fireglow'
Fuchsia fulgens*
Helenium 'Moerheim Beauty'*
Kniphofia caulescens
Lilium tigrinum*
Lonicera 'Gold Flame'*
Mimulus aurantiacus
Nemesia strumosa*
Papaver nudicaule*
Potentilla 'Daydawn'*
Rosa 'Alychmist'
Rosa chinensis 'Mutabilis'
Rosa 'Gloire de Dijon'
Rosa 'Nathalie Nypels'
Rudbeckia hirta 'Rustic Dwarfs'*
Salpiglossis sinuata 'Splash'
Tropaeolum majus 'Alaska'*
Tulipa acuminata
Tulipa 'Generaal de Wet'

Whites
Alcea rosea single white
Anaphalis triplinervis
Anemone blanda 'White Splendour'
Anemone × hybrida 'Honorine
  Jobert'
Aster 'Montecassino'*
Astrantia major
Bergenia 'Silberlicht'
Camellia 'Cornish Snow'*
Campanula lactiflora alba
Campanula persicifolia alba*
Centranthus ruber albus
Choisya ternata
Cistus corbariensis*
Clematis 'Huldine'
Clematis × jouiniana 'Praecox'
Convallaria majalis
Cosmos 'Purity'*
Crambe cordifolia*
Crambe maritima
Crocus 'Bowles' White'
Cyclamen coum album
Dianthus 'Haytor White'
Dianthus 'Musgrave's Pink'
Digitalis purpurea alba
Epilobium glabellum
Escallonia 'Iveyi'
Exochorda macrantha 'The Bride'*
Filipendula vulgaris 'Plena'
Galanthus 'Ophelia'
Galtonia candicans*
Geranium renardii
Helleborus orientalis orientalis
Hesperis matronalis
Iberis sempervirens
Jasminum officinale*
Lathyrus latifolius albus*
Leucojum aestivum 'Gravetye Giant'
Ligustrum lucidum
Lilium candidum
Lilium martagon album
Lilium regale
Lunaria annua

Lunaria annua variegata alba
Lychnis coronaria alba
Lysimachia clethroides
Lysimachia ephemerum
Magnolia salicifolia
Malus sargentii*
Myosotis 'White Ball'
Myrrhis odorata
Myrtus communis*
Narcissus 'Silver Chimes'
Narcissus 'Thalia'
Nicotiana sylvestris
Olearia × scilloniensis
Omphalodes linifolia*
Osmanthus delavayi
Osteospermum barberae 'Blue
  Streak'
Osteospermum ecklonis
Paeonia lactiflora 'Duchesse de
  Nemours'*
Papaver nudicaule*
Phlox maculata 'Omega'
Primula vulgaris 'Alba Plena'
Pyracantha 'Watereri'
Pyrus calleryana 'Chanticleer'
Romneya coulteri
Rosa 'Dupontii'
Rosa 'Mme Alfred Carrière'
Rosa 'Pearl Drift'
Rosa 'White Cockade'*
Rubus cockburnianus
Rubus tridel 'Benenden'*
Silybum marianum
Smilacina racemosa*
Solanum jasminoides 'Album'
Thalictrum aquilegifolium 'White
  Cloud'
Trachelospermum jasminoides*
Tulipa 'Purissima'
Tulipa 'Schoonoord'
Tulipa 'Shirley'
Tulipa 'White Triumphator'
Viburnum 'Anne Russell'*
Viburnum opulus*
Viburnum plicatum 'Mariesii'*
Viburnum tinus 'Eve Price'*
Vinca minor 'Alba Variegata'*
Viola cornuta alba
Wisteria floribunda 'Alba'*

Creamy whites
Aruncus sylvester*
Clematis cirrhosa balearica
Rosa 'Tynwald'
Rosa 'Yvonne Rabier'
Sisyrinchium striatum

GREENS AND FOLIAGE

Green on green
Alchemilla mollis
Angelica archangelica
Bupleurum fruticosum
Buxus suffruticosa
Dryopteris filix-mas

Euphorbia amygdaloides robbiae
Euphorbia characias wulfenii
Euphorbia polychroma*
Fritillaria pontica*
Garrya elliptica*
Hedera colchica 'Paddy's Pride'*
Helleborus corsicus*
Helleborus foetidus 'Wester Flisk'
Heuchera cylindrica 'Greenfinch'*
Hosta plantaginea
Humulus lupulus aureus
Itea ilicifolia
Nectaroscordum siculum
Nicotiana langsdorfii
Nicotiana 'Lime Green'*
Petroselinum crispum
Phyllitis scolopendrium (syn.
  Asplenium scolopendrium)
Polystichum setiferum
Prunus laurocerasus 'Otto Luyken'
Ribes laurifolium
Salvia officinalis 'Icterina'*
Sambucus canadensis 'Aurea'*
Sambucus racemosa 'Plumosa Aurea'
Sarcococca hookeriana digyna

Smyrnium perfoliatum*
Tulipa 'Palestrina'
Tulipa 'Spring Green'
Valeriana phu 'Aurea'
Veratrum album
Zinnia 'Envy'*

Blue-green leaves
Crambe maritima
Eryngium giganteum*
Eryngium × oliverianum
Eucalyptus gunnii*
Euphorbia myrsinites*
Festuca glauca*
Hebe pinguifolia 'Pagei'*
Hosta 'Buckshaw Blue'*
Hosta sieboldiana
Iris pallida pallida
Lavandula angustifolia*
Melianthus major
Nepeta 'Six Hills Giant'
Rosa glauca*
Ruta graveolens 'Jackman's Blue'
Veronica perfoliata*

Silver or grey leaves
Acacia dealbata
Anaphalis triplinervis
Artemisia arborescens
Artemisia 'Powis Castle'
Ballota acetabulosa*
Convolvulus cneorum*
Cyclamen hederifolium*
Cynara cardunculus*
Cytisus battandieri*
Elaeagnus angustifolia*
Elaeagnus × ebbingei 'Limelight'
Helichrysum petiolare*
Iris 'Florentina'
Onopordum acanthium
Potentilla 'Vilmoriniana'*
Salix hastata 'Wehrhahnii'
Santolina chamaecyparissus*
Santolina pinnata neapolitana
Sedum spectabile
Senecio 'Sunshine'*
Stachys byzantina 'Silver Carpet'
Teucrium fruticans
Thymus lanuginosus*
Verbascum olympicum

Variegated white or cream leaves
Azara microphylla 'Variegata'*
Brunnera 'Hadspen Cream'*
Cornus alba 'Elegantissima'
Hosta fortunei albopicta
Hosta fortunei 'Marginata Alba'
Iris pallida 'Variegata'
Kerria japonica 'Variegata'*
Lamium maculatum 'White Nancy'*
Lunaria annua variegata*
Tropaeolum 'Alaska'*
Vinca minor 'Alba Variegata'*
Weigela 'Florida Variegata'

Purple leaves
Ajuga reptans atropurpurea*
Dahlia 'Bishop of Llandaff'
Foeniculum vulgare 'Purpureum'
Fuchsia fulgens*
Heuchera micrantha 'Palace Purple'
Lobelia cardinalis*
Salvia officinalis 'Purpurascens'
Sedum maximum atropurpureum*
Viola labradorica*
Vitis vinifera 'Purpurea'

FURTHER READING

Brickell, Christopher, (editor), *The Royal Horticultural Society Gardeners' Encyclopedia of Plants & Flowers*, London, Dorling Kindersley, 1989
Earle, C. W. and Waterfield, M., *Garden Colour*, London, J. M. Dent, 1922
Hobhouse, Penelope, *Colour in your Garden*, London, Collins, 1985
Jekyll, Gertrude, *Colour Schemes for the Flower Garden*, Woodbridge, Antique Collector's Club, 1987
Thomas, Graham Stuart, *Perennial Garden Plants*, London, J. M. Dent, 1990

ACKNOWLEDGMENTS

The publisher thanks the following photographers and organizations for their kind permission to reproduce the photographs in this book:

1 Andrew Lawson; 2 above left Gary Rogers; 2 above right Neil Holmes; 2 centre left Andrew Lawson; 2 centre right Jerry Harpur/Elizabeth Whiting and Associates; 2 below left Andrew Lawson; 2 below right Jerry Pavia/Garden Picture Library; 5 Michèle Lamontagne; 6-7 Brigitte Thomas (André Eve); 8 Christopher Simon Sykes; 9 Stephen Robson/National Trust Picture Library; 10 Andrew Lawson; 11 Christopher Simon Sykes; 12 left Brigitte Thomas; 12 right Georges Lévêque; 13 Jacqui Hurst/Boys Syndication; 15 above left Andrew Lawson; 15 above right Geoff Dann; 15 below S & O Mathews; 16 Jerry Harpur/Elizabeth Whiting and Associates; 17 left Brigitte Thomas (Mottisfont); 17 right Jacqui Hurst/Boys Syndication; 18 left S & O Mathews; 18 right Jerry Harpur (Reed House, Great Chesterford, Essex); 19 Karl Dietrich-Bühler/Elizabeth Whiting and Associates; 20-1 Marianne Majerus/Garden Picture Library; 22 left Michael Boys/Boys Syndication; 22 right Andrew Lawson; 23 Tania Midgley; 24 Brigitte Thomas; 25 Andrew Lawson; 26 Michael Boys/Boys Syndication; 27 Brigitte Thomas; 28 Brigitte Thomas (The Old Rectory); 29 Andrew Lawson; 30 Michael Boys/Boys Syndication; 31 Brigitte Thomas; 33 Eric Crichton; 34 above and centre Photos Horticultural; 34 below Eric Crichton; 36 above Eric Crichton; 36 centre Tania Midgley; 36 below left Photos Horticultural; 36 below centre and right Eric Crichton; 37 Eric Crichton; 39 left J. E. Robson/The National Trust for Scotland; 39 right Jacqui Hurst/Boys Syndication; 40-1 Brigitte Thomas; 42-4 Andrew Lawson; 45 left Andrew Lawson; 45 right Brigitte Thomas (Chatsworth); 46 Brigitte Thomas (Greencroft); 47 Brigitte Thomas (Turzey); 48 Jerry Pavia/Garden Picture Library; 49 Brigitte Thomas (Mottisfont); 50 left Steven Wooster/Garden Picture Library; 50 below Brigitte Thomas; 51 Jerry Harpur (designer: Peter Place); 53 left Georges Lévêque; 53 right Eric Crichton; 56 Eric Crichton; 58 Michèle Lamontagne; 59 left and centre Eric Crichton; 59 above right and below right Eric Crichton; 59 centre right Andrew Lawson; 61 Eric Crichton; 62-3 Brigitte Thomas (Sissinghurst); 64 left S & O Mathews; 64 right Eric Crichton; 65 Jerry Harpur (Chenies Manor, Buckinghamshire); 66 left John Miller (Ladbroke Estate); 66 right Steven Wooster/Garden Picture Library; 67 left Jerry Harpur (designers: Wayne Winterrowd & Joe Eck); 67 right Brigitte Thomas (The Old Rectory); 68 left Eric Crichton; 68 right MAP; 69 Brigitte Thomas (Sissinghurst); 70 Brigitte Thomas (Poley); 71 Brigitte Thomas; 73 Eric Crichton; 75 Eric Crichton; 76 above and below left Eric Crichton; 76 centre Eric Crichton; 76 above and below right Photos Horticultural; 78 left Eric Crichton; 78 right Andrew Lawson; 79 left Andrew Lawson; 79 right Eric Crichton; 80-1 Neil Holmes; 82 left Andrew Lawson; 82 right Stephen Robson/National Trust Picture Library; 83 Brigitte Thomas (Fairfield); 84 left Andrew Lawson; 84 right Brigitte Thomas; 85 Karl Dietrich-Bühler/Elizabeth Whiting and Associates; 86 Eric Crichton/National Trust Picture Library; 87 left Andrew Lawson; 87 right S & O Mathews; 88 left Brigitte Thomas; 88 right Neil Holmes; 89 Brigitte Thomas; 90 Stephen Robson/National Trust Picture Library; 91 Brigitte Thomas; 93 Eric Crichton; 95 Eric Crichton; 96 above and below left Eric Crichton; 96 centre Andrew Lawson; 96 above and below right Eric Crichton; 98 above Photos Horticultural; 98 below Eric Crichton; 99 Eric Crichton; 100-1 Nick Meers/National Trust Picture Library; 102 Michael Boys/Boys Syndication; 103 Jacqui Hurst/Boys Syndication; 105 above left Ann Kelley/Elizabeth Whiting and Associates; 105 above right Clive Nichols; 105 below Andrew Lawson; 106 Clay Perry; 107 Andrew Lawson; 108-9 Jerry Harpur/Elizabeth Whiting and Associates; 110 left Jacqui Hurst/Boys Syndication; 110 right Elizabeth Whiting and Associates; 111 Brigitte Thomas (André Eve); 113 Photos Horticultural; 114 left and centre Photos Horticultural; 114 right Eric Crichton; 116 Marijke Heuff (Mr & Mrs Groenewegen); 117 above left Photos Horticultural; 117 above right Neil Holmes; 117 below Eric Crichton; 119 left Brigitte Thomas (Vaughan); 119 right Photos Horticultural; 120-1 S & O Mathews; 122 John Glover/Garden Picture Library; 123 left Brian Carter/Garden Picture Library; 123 right Andrew Lawson; 124 S & O Mathews; 125 Brigitte Thomas; 126 left Clive Nichols; 126 right Jerry Harpur (Tintinhull); 127 Clive Nichols; 128 left Andrew Lawson; 128 right Jerry Harpur (The Dingle, Welshpool); 129 Brigitte Thomas (Weeks Farm); 132 above left Photos Horticultural; 132 above and centre right Eric Crichton; 132 below Eric Crichton; 134 left Eric Crichton; 134 centre and right Photos Horticultural; 135 above left Gary Rogers; 135 below left Photos Horticultural; 135 below centre Eric Crichton; 135 below right Photos Horticultural.